ISSUE 02

Berkeley Arts + Design

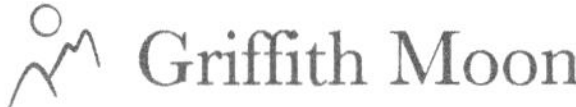

Printed in the United States of America
First Printing, 2018

Published by Griffith Moon
Santa Monica, California
GriffithMoon.com

ISBN 978-0-9998452-3-3
Library of Congress Control Number: 2018938759

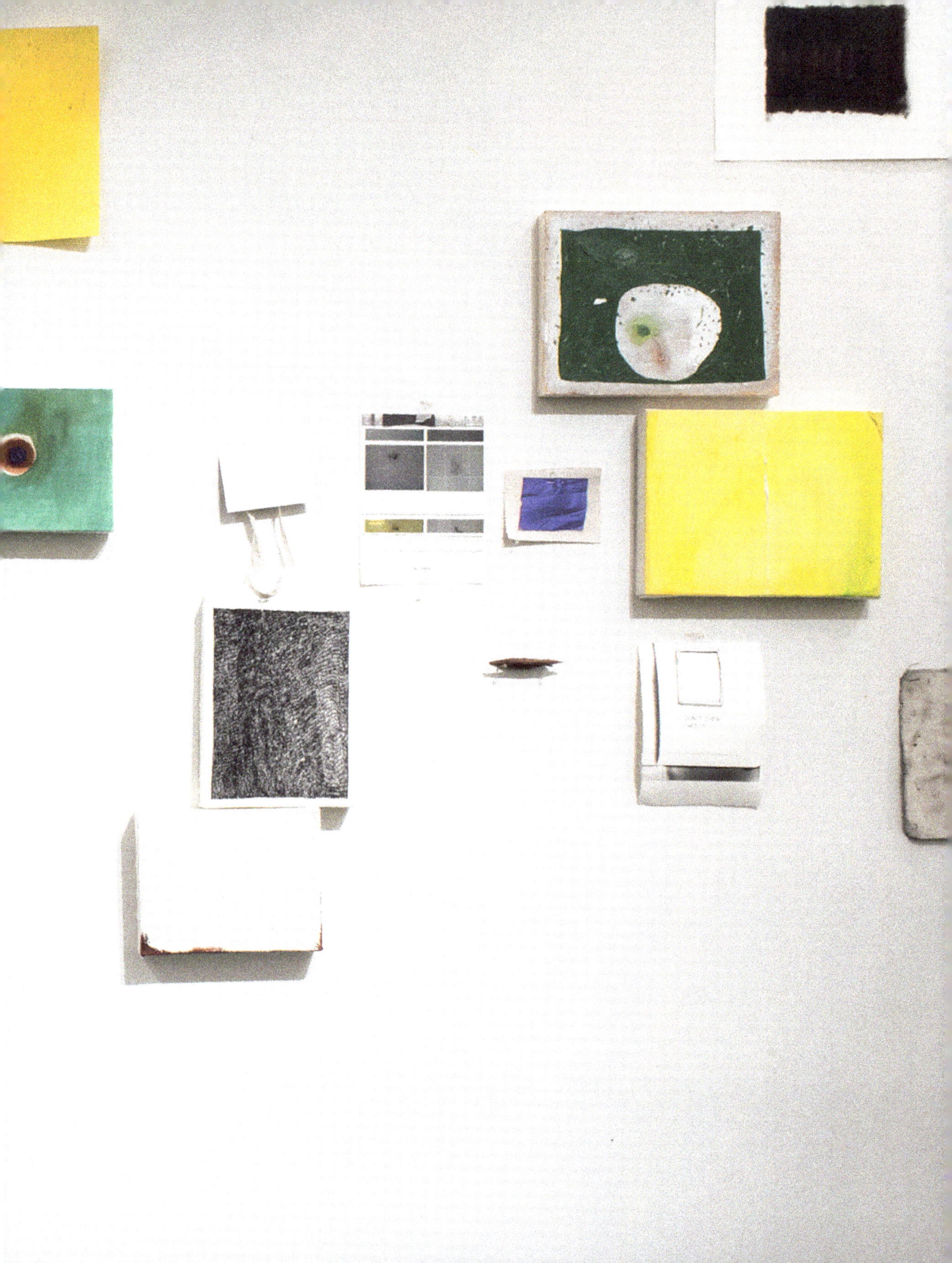

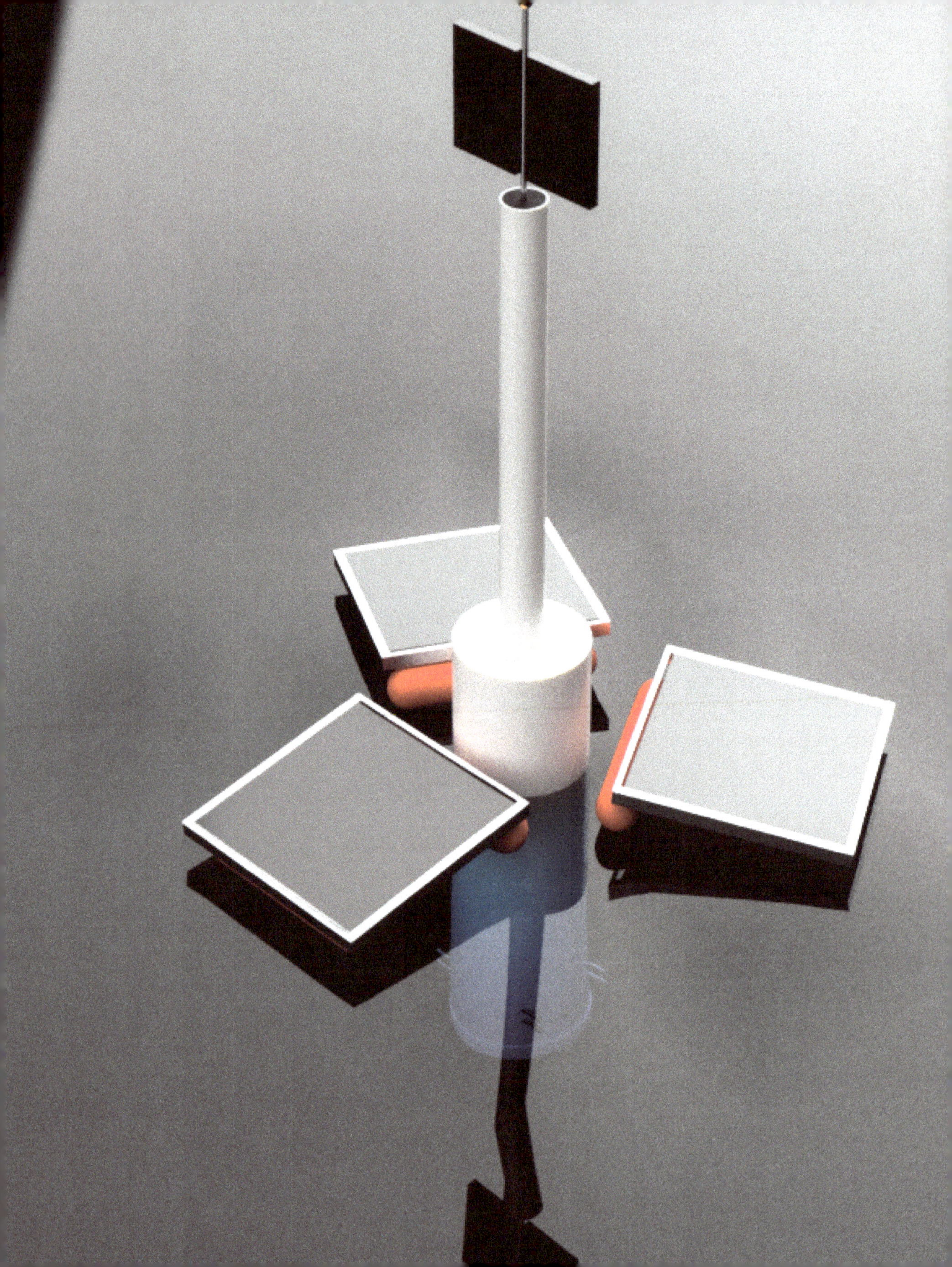

TABLE OF CONTENTS

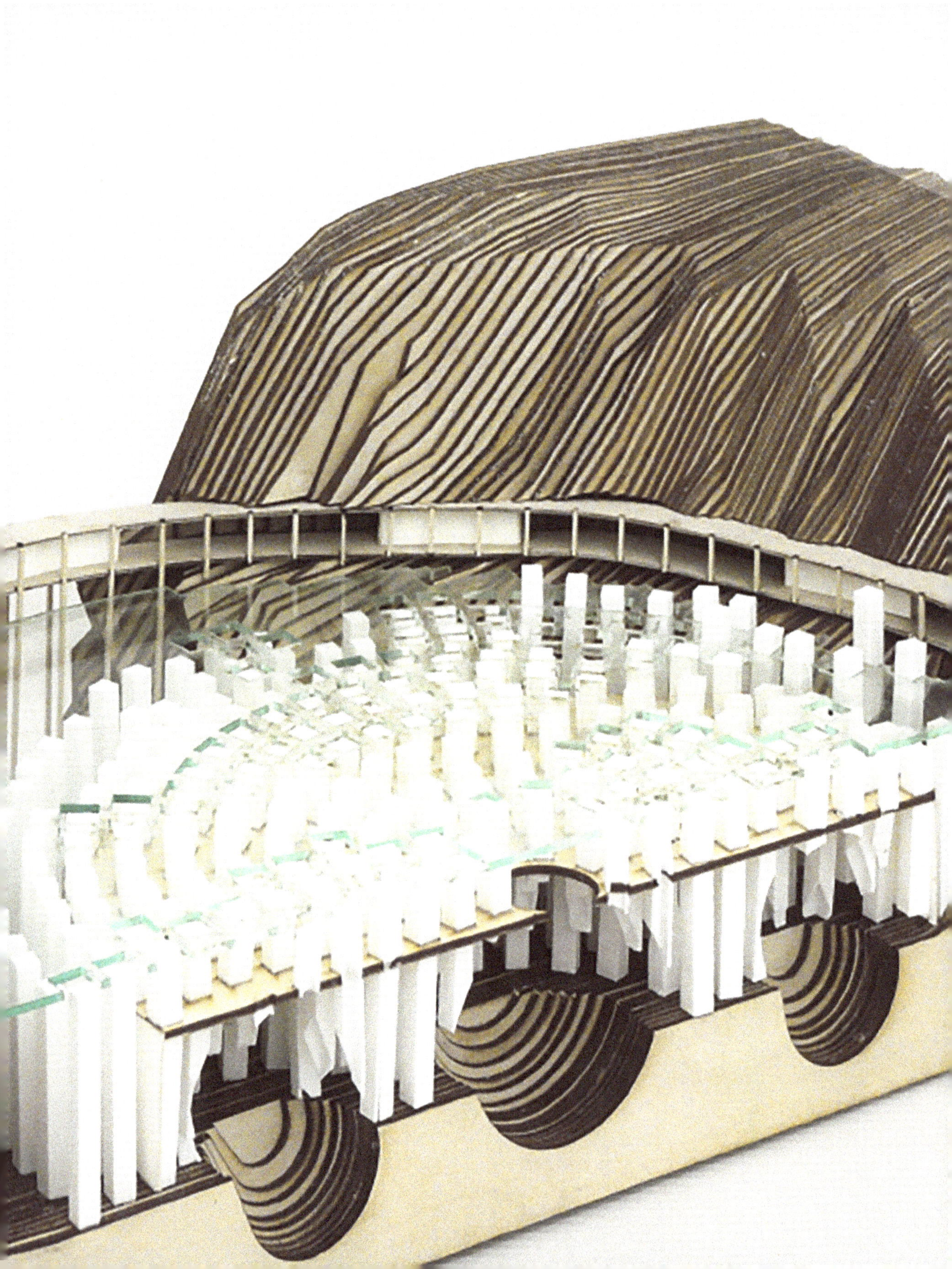

INTRODUCTION

It's been quite a year—for our country, for UC Berkeley, and for the Arts + Design Initiative. We navigated changes in our political landscape and confronted challenges to freedom of speech and freedom of assembly. Meanwhile, as evidenced in the pages before you, our creative students thrived. Whether writing poetry or analyzing fiction, whether working behind the camera or in front of it, on stage or in the wings, with paint or on a computer, the creative works of our students are staggeringly rich and wide-ranging. As they have for 150 years, Berkeley students show us the way forward; their collective imagination is our North Star—for our campus, for the state, and for a globalizing world.

Creativity motors our public research university, and, at the same time, our public research university provides a compelling context for creative making. Unlike traditional art schools or conservatories, Berkeley features a wide range of creative disciplines and genres. Sculptors work next to musicians; musicians work with film-makers; film-makers work with dancers who work with designers who work with poets. Moreover, our artists and designers understand their practice with a deep sense of history and tradition, and with a lens that is both critical and global. They re-engage classic myths; they speculate on creative connection across nations and cultures. You will also find our students nesting creative action within the laboratories of our scientists and testing the parameters of the latest technology. Berkeley activated the values of S.T.E.A.M. (Science, Technology, Engineering, Arts, Math) long before the acronym became trendy. You will find new ideas of how a rigorous S.T.E.A.M. platform yields new functions to solve pressing social problems as well as new prototypes that reconceive what 'functional' can be. Indeed, most importantly, you'll find in this collection evidence, not only of how the creativity transforms a research university, but also what happens when creativity works on behalf of the values of public access and social justice at a university like UC Berkeley. In project after project, you see the results of creativity directed toward the greater good.

This book is Issue Number 2 in what is fast becoming an A + D [Arts + Design] tradition, advancing our mission to unify, fortify, and amplify the tremendous creative culture of UC Berkeley. The projects have been sourced from our wide network of undergraduate programs across the Visual Arts, Performing Arts, Literature, Film,

Media, Architecture, and Engineering Design. While housed in selected departments, you will find that many of these projects cut across genre and medium, challenging the boundaries amongst art forms and breaking boundaries between art and public life. Most students were the recipients of departmental awards or rose to the top in campus-wide contests and juried courses. We also decided to remind ourselves and our readers that 'capstones' only come after students have been exposed to a range of creative forms in the beginning of their undergraduate career; our collection begins with reflections from students in the midst of their first experiences of Berkeley's creative culture, anticipating where those experiences might go. Together, these projects also offer a sampler of the variety and expertise of our faculty and staff; our educators have a tremendous range of creative skills and undying commitment to cultivating new discoveries amongst a next generation of creatives. Indeed, the process of compiling this book is another reminder of their commitment, and we are thrilled to honor the incredible mentorship of the teachers who make this creativity possible on a daily (and often nightly) basis.

As they have for every culture and historical era, the arts and design provided a vehicle for self-expression on our campus; they are the glue by which we build community and with which we create conditions for bracing public dialogue. The arts inspire and provoke; they challenge and provide comfort. Through creative forms, we honor tradition, and we break tradition. Through creative action, we imagine anew and welcome the unexpected.

It is our privilege to celebrate the forms, actions, and expressions of our students—and to encourage them to invent new traditions of their own.

Enjoy, Relish, Cherish.

Fiat Lux and Go Bears,

Shannon Jackson
Associate Vice Chancellor for the Arts and Design
University of California, Berkeley

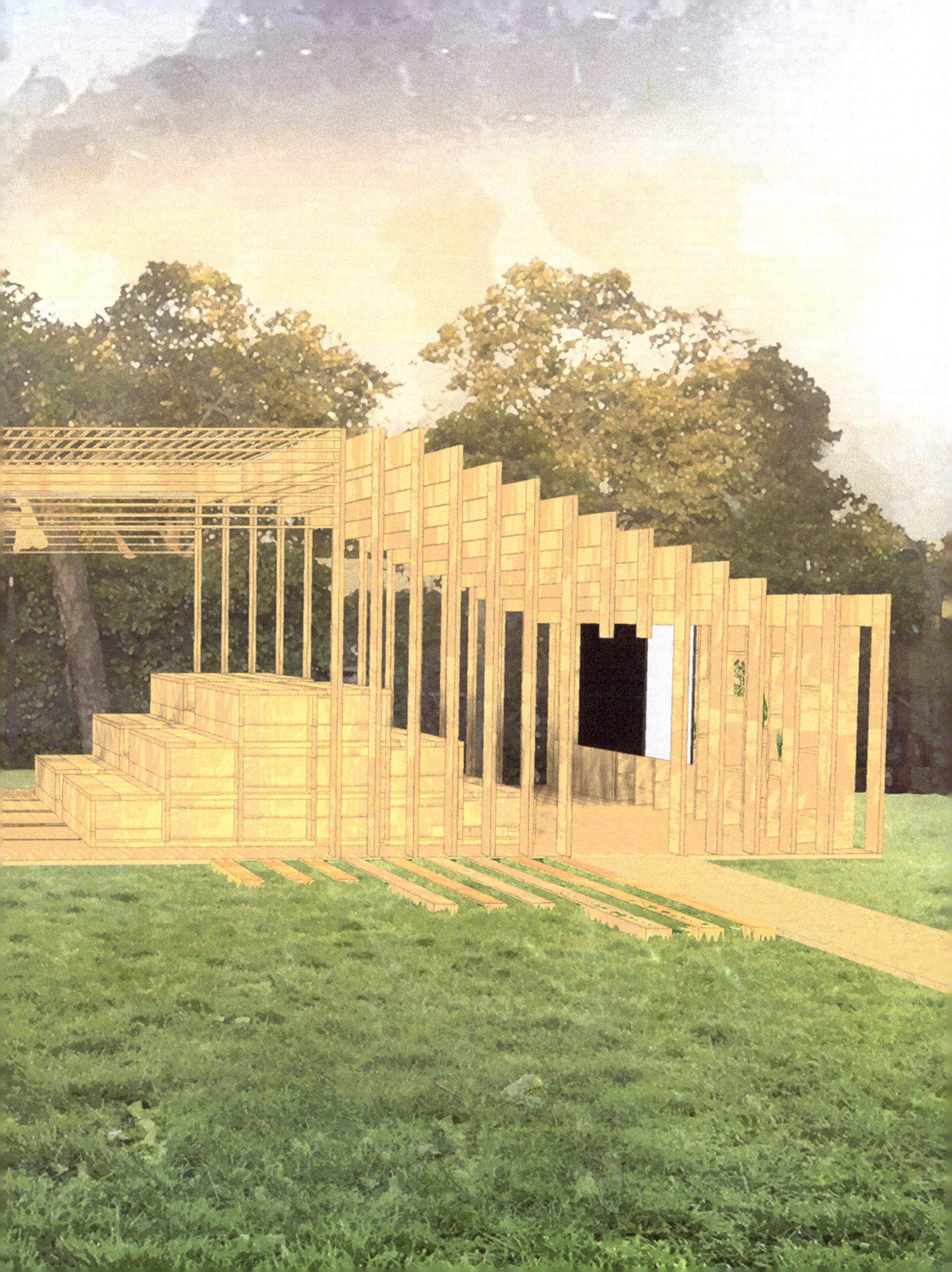

NEW CLASSICS

JI YOUNG JUN
MERISSA MANN
THEODORA SERBANESCU MARTIN
MAYA SHEN
JENNY REMPERT
EDOARDO BENZONI
ALEXANDER BARREIRA
ANDREW RAHMAN

Ji Young Jun

I have chosen to depict the three beasts that block Dante's way; the leopard, lion, and she-wolf realistically. However, I have contained them within the silhouette of Dante's head's profile. With this, I sought to represent the allegory of a person's internal journey toward God, showing that the beasts are not literal beasts but are rather "beasts" of personal sin and internal obstacles that one must overcome with an inward journey. As for the second piece, I chose to depict Francesca and Paolo realistically as Dore did, but I also situated them within the body. This time, they are within a heart. One reason I chose to place them in the human heart is because that is where we symbolically see their particular sin, forbidden love, living. The other reason I chose the heart is to symbolically represent the descent of Dante's journey. His descent through the levels of hell is an allegory, and in turn my descent from the head to the heart represents a part of that journey.

Ji Young Jun
B.A. History of Art, 2017

Faculty Mentor: Henrike Lange, History of Art

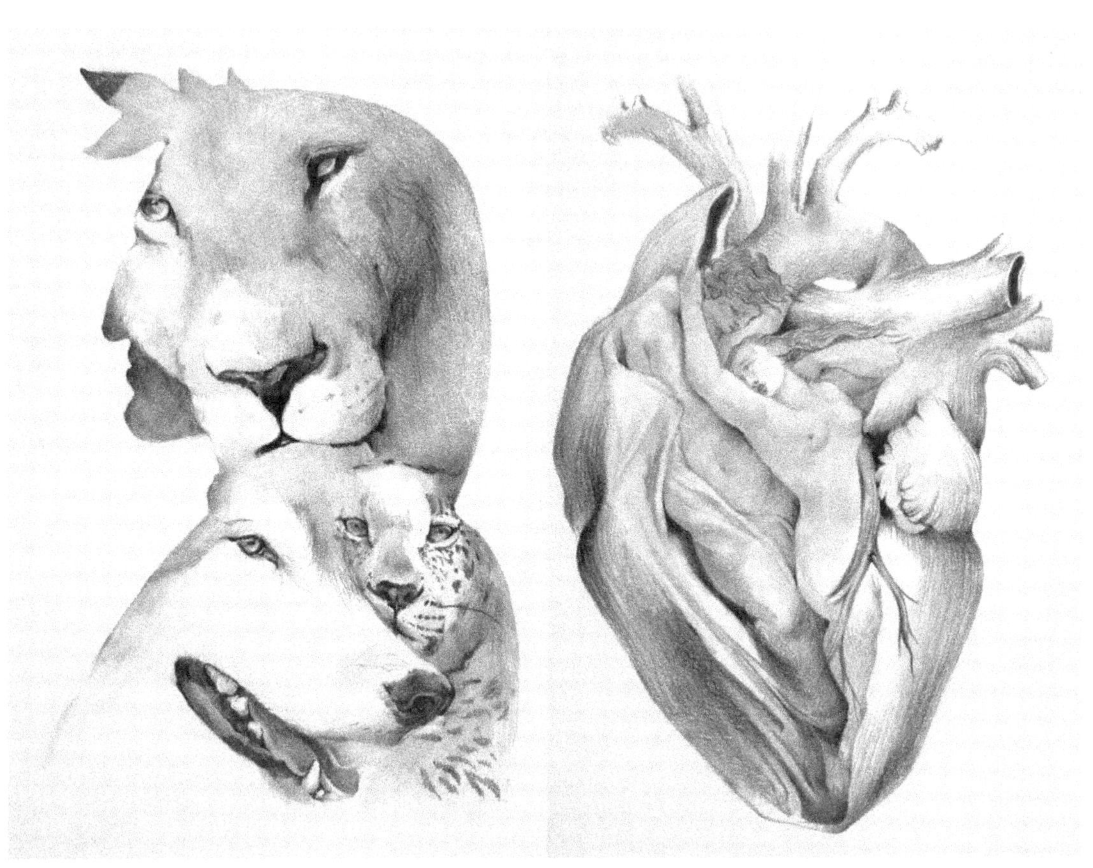

Ji Young Jun, *Canto I, Canto V*, 2016. Pencil on Bristol paper, 14 x 17 inches

Merissa Mann

This custom-designed and hand-built bench functions as a contemporary take on the classic "treasure chest". The mermaid painted on the exterior of the bench pays homage to the fantastical history of the aquatic treasure trove sought by pirates and adventurers alike. The glass mosaic surrounding the figure emulates the reflective quality of water. The top of the bench, padded and covered with elegant black silk, hinges upwards to provide hidden storage space. The bench is ideal for storing pillows, blankets, and other bedroom necessities and treasures. Both aesthetically pleasing and highly functional, the mermaid bench is a one of a kind art object and a new take on a classic image of fantasy.

Merissa Mann
B.A. Art Practice, 2017
Berkeley Design Innovation Certificate, 2017

Faculty Mentor: Jean Paul Bourdier, College of Environmental Design

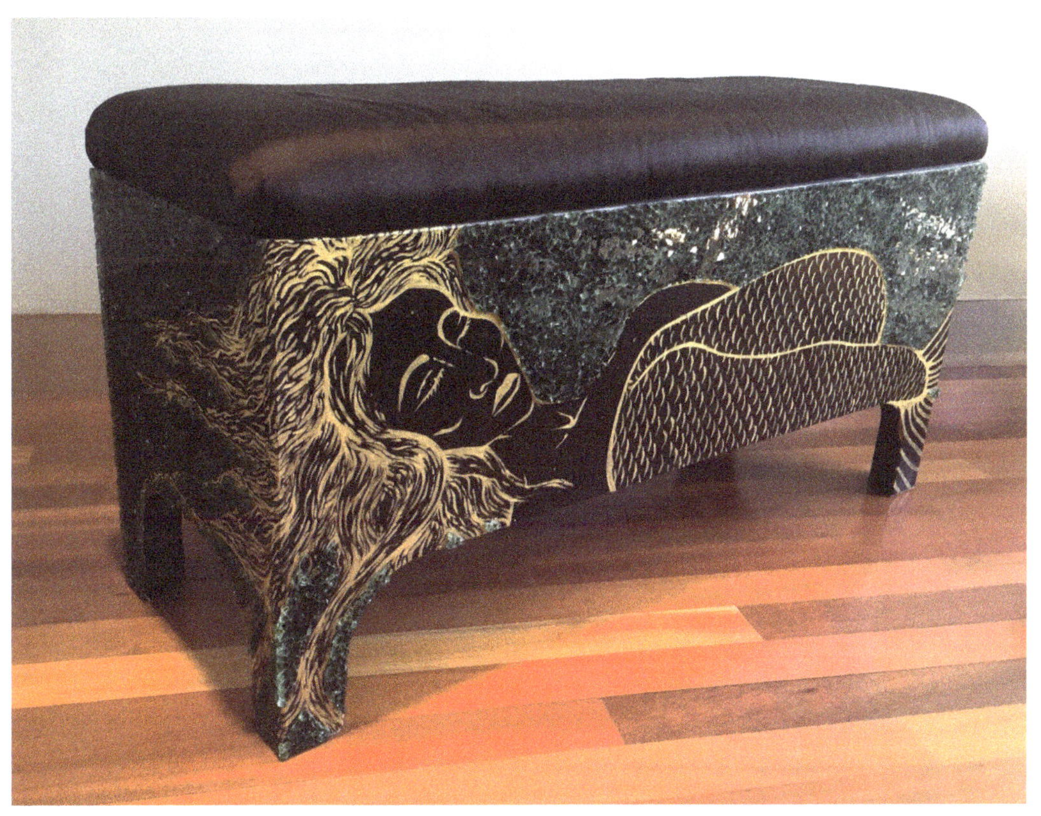

Merissa Mann, *Mermaid Bench*, 2016. Wood, glass, and silk, 48 x 18 x 24 inches.

Theodora Serbanescu Martin

Theodora Serbanescu-Martin graduated from Berkeley in 2016 with BAs and high honors for both Music and English, and a minor for German Studies. Her music thesis, "Brahms's Piano Exercise Mode and the Politics of Friendship" sought to reclassify Brahms's paradoxical virtuosity in relation to his engagement with dialogic music-making. She engages with various pianistic themes such as Brahms, the history of virtuosity, piano pedagogy and schools of the 19th-21st centuries.

Theodora Serbanescu-Martin
B.A. in Music and English
Fall 2016

Faculty Mentor Nicholas Matthew

PART ONE

Brahmsian Pianism, Innig Virtuosity, and the Aesthetics of Effort

Chapter One — Brahms and Paganini: False Antipodes?

I

German or Italian? Virtue or Virtuosity?[1] Throughout the twentieth and twenty-first centuries, Brahms's *Paganini* Variations have endured a reception dogged by a banal rhetoric of binaries. "It seems to me," wrote the American art critic James Huneker in 1899,

> that the pièce de résistance of the Brahms piano music is the Paganini Variations; those famous, awesome, o'ertoppling, huge, fantastic, gargoylean variations erected, planned and superimposed by Brahms upon a characteristic theme of Paganini.
>
> Brahms and Paganini! Was ever so strange a couple in harness? Caliban and Ariel, Jove and Puck. The stolid German, the vibratile Italian! Yet fantasy wins, even if we brewed in a homely Teutonic kettle. Brahms has taken the little motif—a true fiddle motif—of Paganini, and tossed it ball-wise in the air, and while it spiral spins and bathes in the blue, he cogitates, and his thought is marvelously fine spun. Webs of gold and diamond spiders and the great round sun splashing about, and then deep divings into the bowels of the firmament and growling and subterene rumblings, and all the while the poor *maigre* Paganini, a mere palimpsest for the terrible old man of Hamburg, from whose pipe wreathed musical smoky metaphysics, and whose eyes are fixed on the Kantean categories. The diabolical variations, the last word in the technical literature of the piano, are also vast spiritual problems. To play them requires fingers of steel, a heart of burning lava and the courage of a lion. You see, these variations are an obsession with me.[2]

By this time, distinctions between the Italianate and the Germanic, surface and depth, play and work, were longstanding tropes of mid-century anti-virtuosity critiques, voiced influentially by Robert Schumann and, later, Eduard Hanslick, to name a couple. And, as Dana Gooley notes, the increasing dominance of "symphonic" values in self-consciously serious concert venues at the expense of instrumental virtuosity was one of the stories of the nineteenth century whoseconsequences are still with us.[3] For Huneker, then, "*maigre* Paganini" merely flirts with some manuscript paper, while the "terrible old man of Hamburg" scribbles all over it with his corrective quill, elevating its flimsy substance into something more commensurate with his smoke-wreathed Kantean metaphysics. Huneker gives us an early version of the stereotype of the "serious bearded Brahms," whose music, as Anna Scott observes in her 2014 dissertation *Romanticizing Brahms,* is considered today antithetic to "the canon's more virtuosic warhorses and quixotic rhapsodies," and whose "restrained, stoic, portentous and modestly powerful" style demands interpretations shaped by the "aesthetic ideology of control," largely a construct of twentieth-century performance practice.[4] Yet this modernist version of Brahms surely counts among its ancestors even Schumann's famous "Neue Bahnen" of 1853, which set up the inevitable eclipse of the "not-so-serious" Brahms (if there is such a thing), and made later works such as the *Paganini* Variations so hard for generations of musicians and critics to grasp.

Indeed, there was no Brahmsian pipe (or—perhaps even more emblematic—no weighty Teutonic beard) when a charming, svelte 29-year-old Johannes began work on these variations. This young heartthrob was, as his *Schatzkästlein des Jungen Kreislers* diary reveals, more often drifting away in Novalean dreams than keeping his eyes fixed on Kantean categories. And most importantly, the ostensibly serious North Germany was excitedly planning, for the first time in 1862, to relocate to charming Vienna.[5] Four years later, following his first performances of Op. 35 in Basel and Winterthür, journalist, literary critic and amateur singer Josef Viktor Widmann describes him like this:

> [Brahms]... immediately gave the impression of a powerful individuality, not only by means of his mighty piano-playing, which cannot be compared with even the greatest of merely brilliant virtuosity, but also through his personal appearance. It is true, the short square figure, the almost straw blond hair, the jutting lower lip which lent the *beardless* youth a slightly sarcastic expression, were conspicuous and hardly prepossessing peculiarities; but his entire aspect was permeated by *strength.* The broad lion-like chest, the herculean shoulders, the mighty head at times tossed back

energetically when playing, the contemplative, beautiful brow glowing as if by an inner light, and the Germanic eyes framed in blond lashes and radiating a marvellously fiery glance, they all betrayed an artistic personality brimming to the very fingertips with genius. There was also a certain confidence of victory in his countenance, the glowing cheerfulness of a spirit happy in the execution of his art, and without turning my eyes from the young master who gripped the keys with such power, there came to mind Iphigenia's words on the Olympian gods...[6]

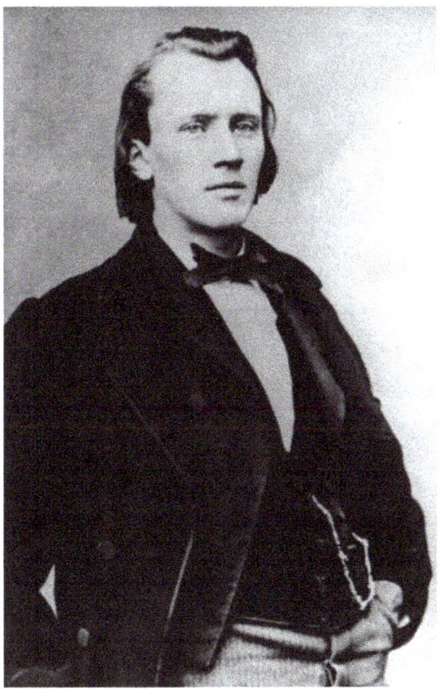

Figure 1: A young Brahms from the 60s

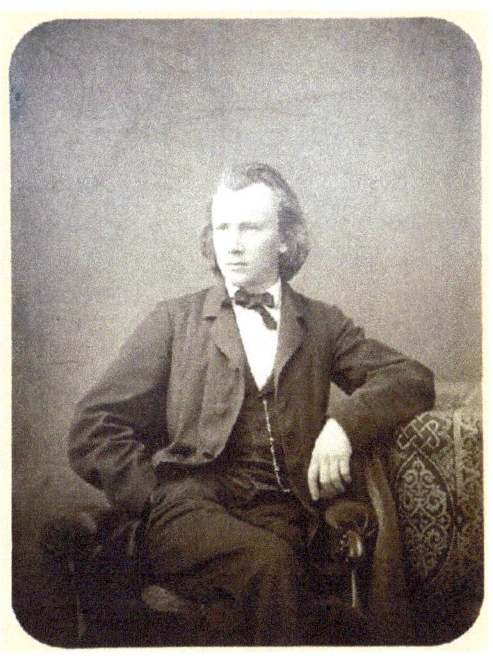

Figure 2: Brahms in Vienna, ca. 1866/67

No other image of Brahms captures his muscular strength (and beardlessness!) quite so poetically. And even though Widmann's snapshot of monumental strength is incongruent with the better-known descriptions of Brahms's supposedly awkward pianism, it is worth noting how the inevitable "merely" appears in conjunction with the "brilliant virtuosity" of his contemporaries.[7] Even in the 1860s, it seems, Brahmsian virtuosity was a precarious thing—a rhetorically contorted turning-inward of the "mere" virtuosity Brahms's contemporaries would overly embody. In Widmann's eyes, Brahms doesn't just sweat; his "contemplative brow" glows "as if by an inner light." From his body flows not empty dazzle, but fiery German *Genie*.

Brahms's Teutonic seriousness, deep and intellectual, cannot be fully externalized; his is an *innig* virtuosity. For all that, it is still a kind of virtuosity. Indeed, Widmann divides his analysis equally between the Brahmsian *geistig* and muscular corporeal. To present-day piano students, routinely exposed to the myth of the powerfully serious, weighty Brahms, it may seem surprising that there was not only a time when Brahms was clean-shaven, as Figures 1 and 2 prove, but that he had the body of an "Olympian god," and performed not awkward "spirited sketches" of difficult pieces, but played with a "certain confidence of victory in his countenance."[8]

But to recover a *Brahms ohne Bart*, to use Jan Swafford's playful term, is only a first step towards reclaiming the virtuoso Brahms.[9] Using the *Paganini* Variations, Brahms's most technically daunting solo piano work, as a point of departure, I seek here to prove that Brahms's pianism rivaled that of the greatest pianists of his day, and to reconsider the arguments of scholars as various as Roger Moseley, Charles Rosen, and Bernard Sherman, who have, to varying degrees, reinscribed the idea that Brahms's pianism was "awkward." To do so, Part One aims to reconstruct the Brahmsian body, and to position his "*innig* virtuosity" amid the range of more familiar Romantic bodies and virtuosities. This will involve, in Chapter One, further examining the reception of Op. 35 (and in the process correcting two widely accepted but erroneous facts about the conception and earliest performance of the piece). Although my argument has many points of contact with recent attempts by scholars and performers to revise the dominant image of the "serious bearded Brahms," I do not aim only to reconstruct an alternative interpretive aesthetic or "historically performance practice," as Scott does when she infers how Brahms would have played from her valuable synthesis (and duplication) of various early recorded account of his works. In Chapter Two of Part One, I also want to understand, via accounts of Brahms's teaching and practice, how the Brahmsian body was expressed and formed at the keyboard, and, crucially, to explore the friendly and unfriendly relations between different pianistic bodies across historical eras, which have encountered one another through Brahms's music.

ENDNOTES

1 For a book whose title happens to match my question, see Jane O'Dea, *Virtue or Virtuosity?: Explorations in the Ethics of Musical Performance* (Westport, CT: Greenwood Press, 2000).

2 James Huneker, *Mezzotints in Modern Music; Brahms, Tschaikowsky, Chopin, Richard Strauss, Liszt and Wagner* (New York: C. Scribner's Sons, 1899), 56.

3 See Dana A. Gooley, "The Battle Against Instrumental Virtuosity in the Early Nineteenth Century," in *Franz Liszt and His World*, ed. Christopher Howard. Gibbs and Dana A. Gooley (Princeton: Princeton University Press, 2006), 75–106. For a discussion of these values in today's concert halls, see Janet Malcolm's analysis of Anthony Tommasini's compare-contrast review of Murray Perahia and Yuja Wang's performances of Beethoven's *Hammerklavier* in Janet Malcolm, "Yuja Wang and the Art of Performance," *The New Yorker* (15 September, 2016). http://www.newyorker.com/magazine/2016/09/05/yuja-wang-and-the-art-of-performance. Accessed 4 December 2016.

4 Anna Scott, *Romanticizing Brahms: Early Recordings and the Reconstruction of Brahmsian Identity.* (PhD diss., Leiden University, 2014), v–vi.

5 For more background on Brahms's back-and-forth moves in and out of Vienna, see Michael Musgrave, "Years of Transition: Brahms and Vienna 1862–1875," in *The Cambridge Companion to Brahms* (Cambridge, U.K.: Cambridge University Press, 1999), 31–50.

6 Jan Swafford, Johannes Brahms: A Biography (New York: Vintage Books, 1999).

7 For a discussion of Brahms's "awkward" pianism, see Charles Rosen, "Brahms. Brahms: Classicism and the Inspiration of Awkwardness," in *Critical Entertainments: Music Old and New* (Cambridge, MA: Harvard University Press, 2000), 162–200. See also Michael Musgrave and Bernard D. Sherman, *Performing Brahms: Early Evidence of Performance Style* (Cambridge, U.K.: Cambridge University Press, 2003), especially chapters 1, 2, 4, 7 and 11.

8 For a complex analysis of Brahms's performances of his own pieces, including his Second Concerto, (and his friends' review of their "sketchiness"), see Roger Moseley, "Between Work and Play: Brahms as Performer of His Own Music," in *Brahms and His World*, ed. Kevin Karnes and Walter Frisch (Princeton University Press, 2009), 137–166. Moseley's argument about Brahmsian pianism—the most nuanced to date—does work against the stereotype that Brahms was not a good pianist, but, because it focuses on late (post-beard) performances and on Brahms's somehow dwindling virtuosity, further reinstates the stereotypes.

9 Swafford, xiii.

VISUAL ARTS

Maya Shen

Illustrating Dante *is the first page, Canto 1, of my depiction of Dante Alighieri's* Divine Comedy: Inferno *in a comic or graphic novel format. This piece was my final project for the class Introduction to Italian Renaissance Art, and was inspired by the connections I made between the class and my own prior knowledge and experiences. I wanted to bring the flexibility and accessibility of the comic and graphic novel genre to* Divine Comedy, *an incredibly famous piece of writing that is not easily read or understood due to its textual difficulty and deep hidden ideas. My idea was to not only illustrate it, but to create a piece that could tell the story in an understandable, straight-forward way. Just like the beginning line, "in the middle of the journey of our life," encourages the reader to recognize the symbolic purpose of the protagonist and his situation in regards to their own life, I hope that my piece would allow for others to be able to enjoy and live Dante's* Divine Comedy: Inferno *themselves.*

Maya Shen
B.A. Cognitive Science, 2020

Faculty Mentor: Henrike Lange, History of Art

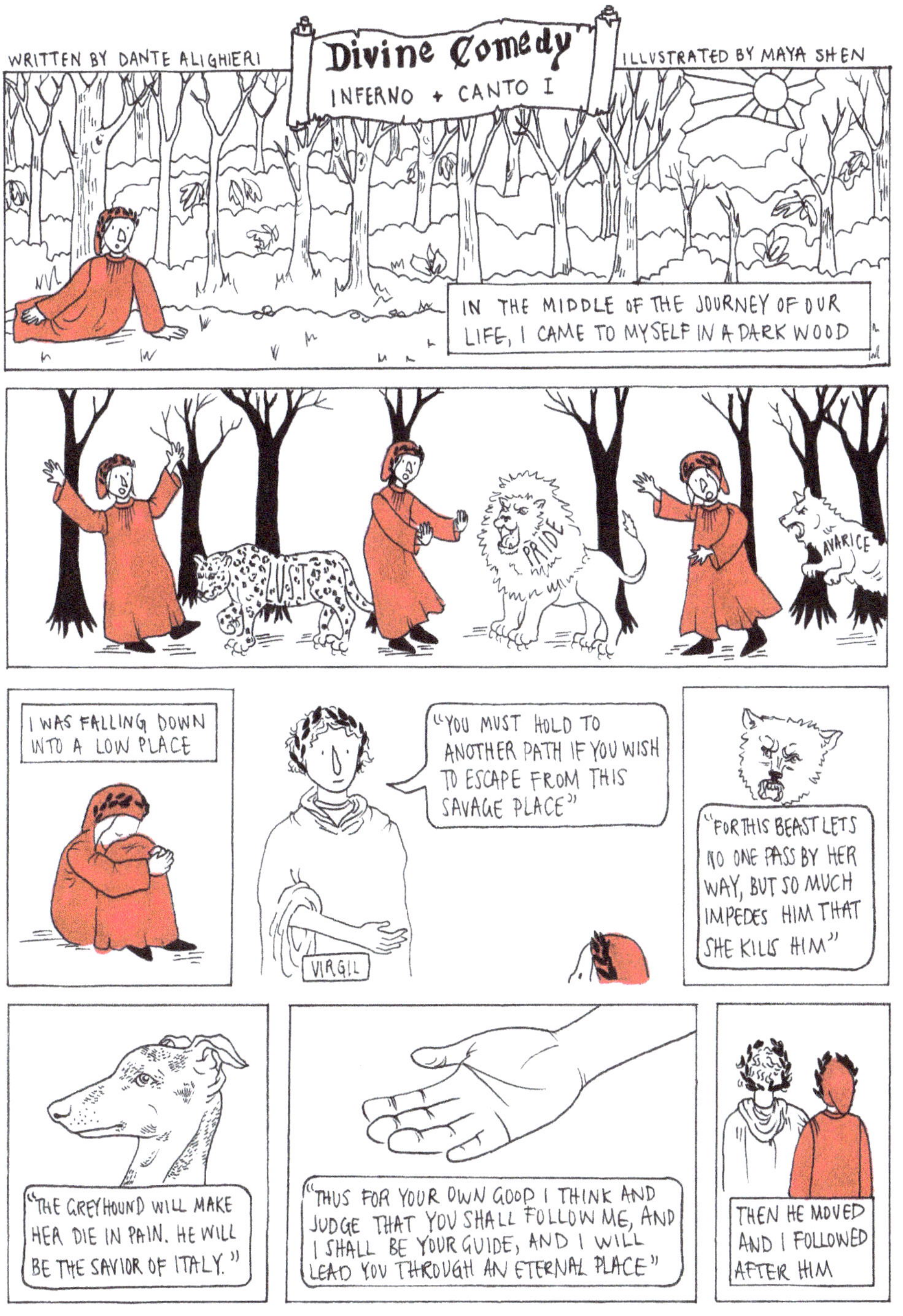

Maya Shen, *Illustrating Dante*, 2015. Ink on paper, 11 x 8.5 inches.

Jenny Rempert

The idea of an "ideal city" is vital in understanding the thoughts and values of Renaissance-era Italy. It combines the humanist desire for logic and organization and proposes that this desire manifests into a physical space. This physical space would be pristine, efficient, and could be easily defined and categorized by simple geometric shapes. The logic and geometry evident in the idea of an "ideal city" can also be connected to Vitruvius and Leonardo Da Vinci's investigations of the human body. Vitruvius was able to logically relate the parts of the body into ratios and geometric shapes, and Leonardo took inspiration from his work and illustrated this in the form of his Vitruvian Man. Both the ideal city and the Vitruvian Man explore the concept of perfection and logic, and both are powerful evidence of the desire for organization and order in the Renaissance period.

Jenny Rempert
B.A. Architecture, 2020

Faculty Mentor: Henrike Lange, History of Art

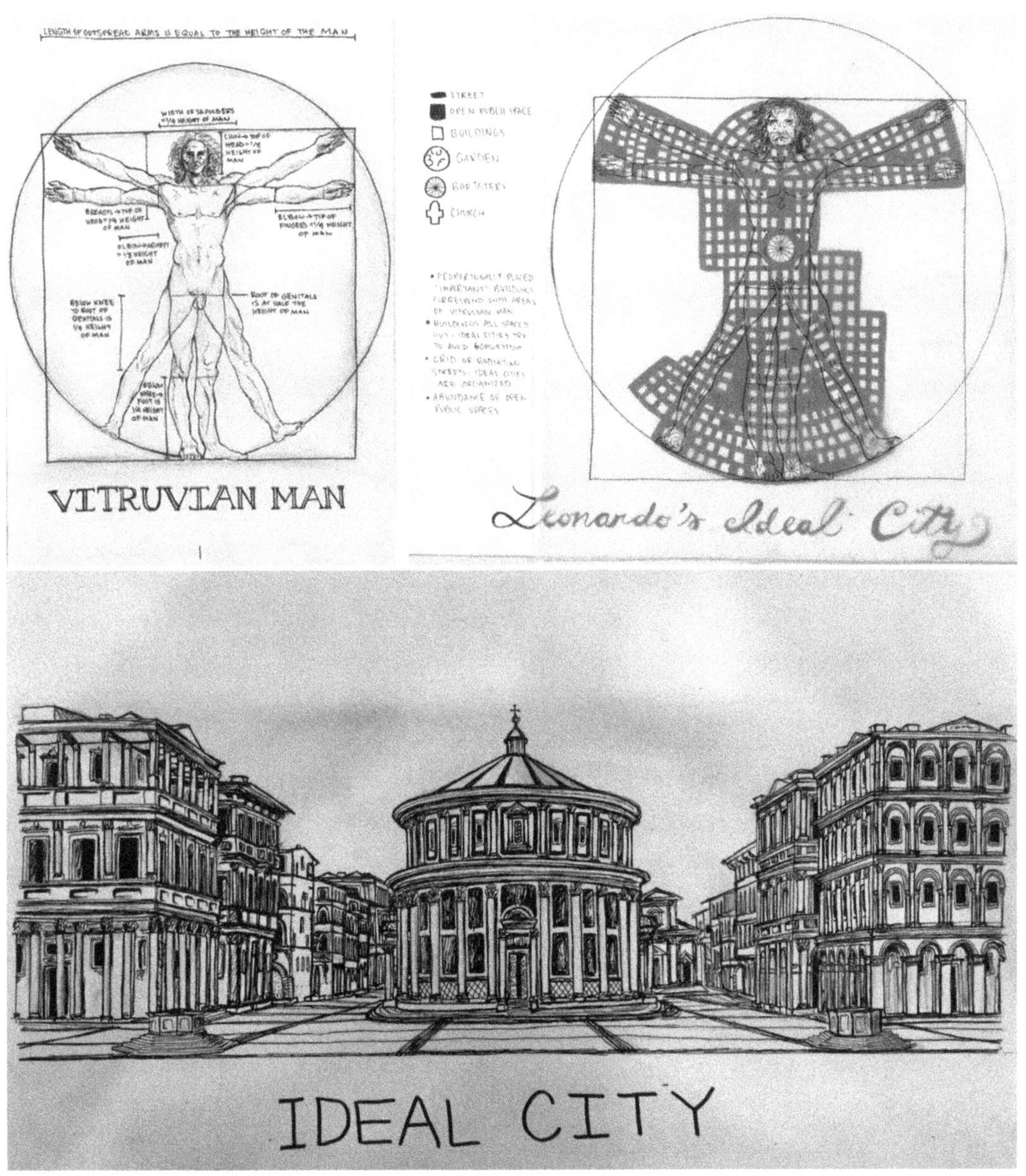

Jenny Rempert, *Idealism in Man and City*, 2016. Pen on paper, 6 x 6 inches, 16 x 12 inches, 10 x 6 inches.

Edoardo Benzoni

The Cherry Orchard *by Anton Chekhov is the story of a Russian aristocratic family that returns to their childhood home during the turn of the 20th century where their lives are turned upside-down when they are unable to sustain their materialistic and wealthy status.*

In the production, I played the character of Leonid Gayev, the eccentric and talkative uncle, who owns the family estate and represents the decadent aristocratic lifestyle who then is rendered helpless due to the social change in Russia. Gayev plays the part of the comedic relief through his extreme optimism, sentimentality and youthful innocence.

The most challenging aspect of preparing to play Gayev was discovering how differently he moves, talks and behaves to myself. I used the Laban technique, which is an analysis of movement used for dancers that we learn in our acting classes at Berkeley to help find Gayev's expression through movement. The opportunity to play such an iconic character in Chekhov's world while getting to work with industry professionals was my greatest experience at UC Berkeley.

Edoardo Benzoni
B.A. Theater, Dance and Performance Studies, 2017
Roselyn Schneider Eisner Prize for Continuing Creative Achievement, 2017

Faculty Mentor: Lura Dolas, Theater, Dance and Performance Studies

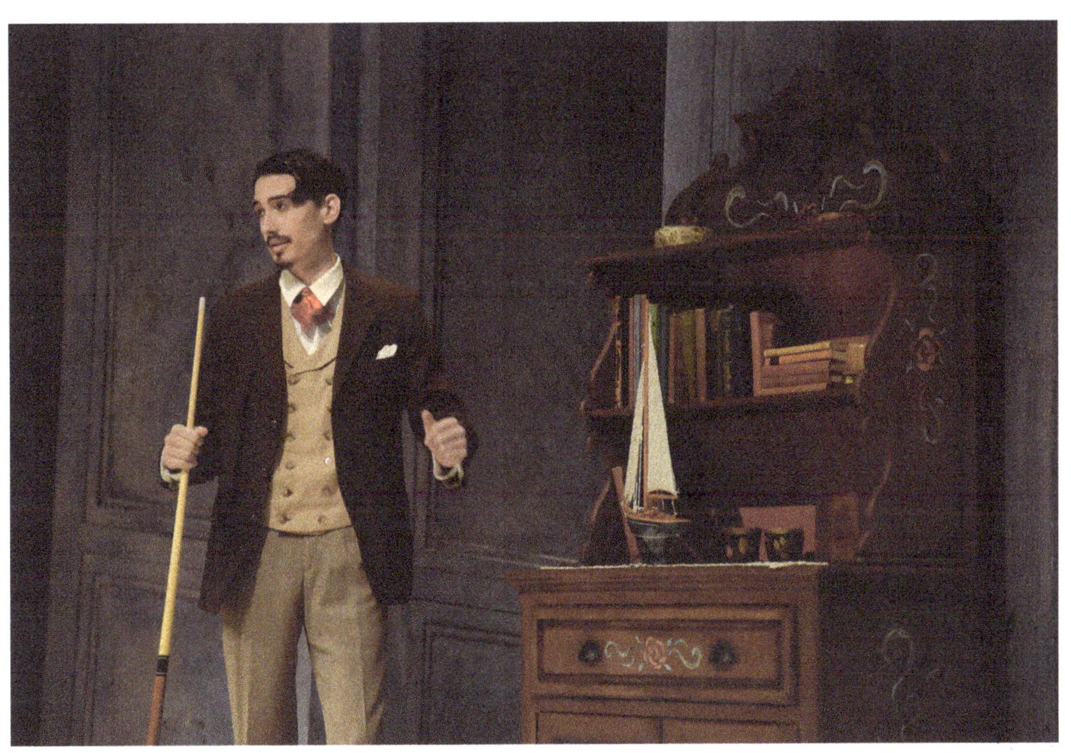

Edoardo Benzoni, *The Cherry Orchard*, 2015. Live performance.

Alexander Barreira

Alexander Barreira is a senior at UC Berkeley majoring in English. He was previously a news editor at the Daily Californian *and works as a reporter from the Chancellor's basement. Since September 2017 he has studied at Waseda University in Tokyo and currently interns at the* Japan Times.

Alexander Barreria
B.A. in English Literature
Spring 2018

Faculty Mentor Jeffery Knapp

Langtry as Entertainment, Aspiration

Lillie Langtry is the most noticeable element of mass entertainment in Vinegarroon, yet her presence fulfills a central function to the identity of the settlement in many ways. The collage of images behind the bar are a jarring image in the first shot of the bar's interior, dominating the wall to suggest the ubiquity of mass entertainment's appeal even to the far fringes of civilization. Yet Bean's relationship to Lillie reconfigures the typical relationship of the consumer to mass entertainment. The pictures behind the bar are not typical entertainment fodder, but rather ads to sell soap (unsuccessful ones, judging by the men in Vinegarroon). It's surprising then that Bean is so enamored, having never seen Lillie on stage, because he treats her picture with the special recognition and intimacy of an art with recognizable aura. Elevating the ads in this way, Bean imbues the ads with his own significance and thus reconstitutes them as an instrument of local culture. We see the implications of this in the very first bar scene, in the tussle over whether or not to toast to Lillie Langtry. On the one hand, Lillie serves as a necessary presence for a settlement that has no women, and provides a common figure of worship in the same way that mass entertainment does on a national scale. The difference is that here she functions as a means to reinforce the antagonistic identity of the cattlemen towards outsiders. So it's understandable that a man who shot Lillie Langtry's poster was hauled out "feet first" and that even when the film's first unfortunate guest compliments Lillie, he is thrown out—one can only claim relation to Lillie Langtry in in the specifically authorized way dictated by Bean. This power only works so long as Lillie exists in image-only. While her person is inaccessible Bean retains creative control over her likeness. It is his fundamental misunderstanding of this dynamic that Hardin exploits, and that dooms Bean. Thus in Vinegarroon mass culture is co-opted to enforce a local identity and its political ramifications, opposed to its original commercial purpose. However there is a suggestion that such power can only exist tentatively in relation to mass culture, on the fringes of civilization.

Hardin takes advantage of Bean through exploiting the fact that Langtry, as a figure of mass culture, belongs to no one. But Lillie represents more than a pretty face to Bean—she represents an aspirational and defensible ideal associated with his confederate past. She's not "Lillie" but "The Jersey Lilly" a configuration that abstracts her person and is suspiciously close to the "southern belle," which fits how she looks as an English actress of high culture. Bean's glory days were at Chickamauga, the Confederate army's greatest defensive victory in the western theater, a fact that should be considered significantly for the Civil War is never far from the minds of

Bazin's Western, which he says have built it up as a kind of "odyssey" (148). In spite of history, Bean hangs onto this confederate identity. The scabbard that he will be "buried with" sits above his collage of Lillie. Bean swears on this civil war relic for the promise of an artifact of Lillie's, suggesting they fulfill the same purpose for him. A tie to the old way of life is more important to him than the new order; he says about the lock "I'd rather own it than the state of Texas." When he goes to the theater to finally meet her he wears his confederate uniform as a way to honor her and also to present her with the most dignified image of himself—not that he is a veteran or that he fought, but that he represents this loyalty, this gallantry. And of course with his posse and scabbard in tow, he is ready to die should he encounter trouble there.

The Space of the Theater

Bean's entry into the theater space marks the beginning of his disillusionment from the access he imagines he has to Lillie's aura. Before the ultimate gun battle this plays out in Bean's attempts to preserve a private connection to her public performance. We don't know what would have happened if it was her and not Hardin when the curtain rolls up, but his actions imply that he hoped for a moment of recognition from Lillie herself. He wears his best clothing and sits in the front row, refusing his 'assigned' seat, and as an extra measure moves his chair to the middle of the aisle. By buying and then burning all the tickets, Bean imagines he attains a greater stake in the performance than he does. But as he chooses his seat, Wyler pulls the camera back in a crane shot that emphasizes the theater's immensity and Bean's diminuity within that space. He is learning that the theater is a more totalizing space in that now there are rules dictating how the entertainment is to be enjoyed. Bean is a conductor figure in Vinegarroon with a personal part in Lillie's presentation, but here the grid-pattern of chairs and curtain mark off his potential as an anonymous consumer. Nor is he able to achieve the privacy he desires—the orchestra sits between him and the stage, and the conductor condescends obviously when he talks to Bean. The most telling image is a return to a wall of ads, a reference to the barroom collage, but here they are someone else's arrangement and their commercial implication is unavoidable. What Bean longs for is an unmediated experience intimately connected to his nostalgic past, but Hardin's substitution for Lillie on stage is the final indication that Bean is no longer in control of the story. The dominant form of entertainment is personified in Hardin's body against the landscape on the stage, and in the close-up that hides the stage's unreality. When Gary Cooper exits the stage into the audience, it is as if to complete the movement of our first image of him riding toward the audience so that now he bursts through the screen to impose the order he's been called by different forces to assure.

The final duel acts as a kind of performance art, a show of its own. As the fight starts the scene cuts to Bean's men outside, who joke: "the war's on!" and "Wish I was in there to see that show." It's unclear whether the references to the show are knowing or ironic, but they demonstrate the insularity and the transformative effect of the theater, a refiguration of war as entertainment.The effect of the fighting is to replace the scheduled performance with one of their own, clearing out the orchestra and actors. The confined space produces a comic effect, in the hustling of the orchestra or the awkwardness of the shooting. When Bean tells Hardin, "you stopped the show" it brings to mind the various levels of performances going on. The effect of the gunfight is both to doom Bean but also to open up a new possibility for his relationship to Lillie—whereas before he would have watched her as an audience member, from the chaos that ensued he gets the chance to go backstage and see her face to face.

It's this moment that makes Bean successful and solidifies his legend, but it also signals the limited potential of the legacy he represents. If Bean is to stand for the Texas that longs for connection with its nostalgic past, it's only at the cost of his life and for a fleeting moment that he can realize something close. He is a martyr for the Texas that is gone and must never again be, he suffers the consequence of foolish attempts to cling to it. Hardin's generous actions at the end then are a way of smoothing over the transition of power, between an ugly version of Texas, soaked in confederate mythos, to the hope of a conciliatory transition from a locally-insular to nationally-expansive stance on the past. And so it makes sense that as Hardin leaves the theater to return Bean's sword, the shadow of a curtain falls over the scene, leading to a parallel transition into the map of Texas. With the past buried, the future can begin on fertile grounds.

But the final scene, while nostalgic and optimistic about the future of Texas, solidifies the troubling substitution of history for style depicted over the course of the film. While Texas's mythic past was represented by real-legend Bean in the title cards, now it's Hardin who carries the torch: "What did I tell you...it's the promised land. Someday Texas is going to be the biggest, the finest." And so this new frontier, offering the illusion of fresh soil, has in fact already been settled in our minds by the heroes we want to see—in Cole galloping gallantly, in his chivalrous acceptance of a new life, an admirable man to aspire to, but not the man who the film entirely wishes to commit us to. Instead, in the ambiguity the film encourages between Bean and Hardin, we're to recognize the importance of the transitory moment occurring: not in the settled conflict of homesteaders and cattlemen, but the never-ending battle over the ways we choose to mythologize the outcome. Vinegarroon demonstrates the importance of these style allegiances to our group identity as a settlement and as a nation, and in the death of its hero, Bean, the film suggests that this local configuration has been displaced for a national one. The kinds of histories permissible and the place we go to find them have shifted, and though in Hardin and Cole's moment of teamwork there's hope for a reconciliation of their two identities, the looming intrusion of the theater suggests otherwise—that borders have been imposed on the imagination of who we are.

Works Cited

Bazin, André. What Is Cinema?, Volume Vol. 2 : Volume II (1). Berkeley, US: University of California Press, 2004. ProQuest ebrary. Web. 28 April 2017.

Crowther, Bosley. "The Screen in Review; "The Westerner'." Rev. of *The Westerner*. *New York Times* 25 Oct. 1940: n. pag. *The New York Times*. The New York Times Co. Web. 28 Apr. 2017.

Miller, Gabriel. *William Wyler : The Life and Films of Hollywood's Most Celebrated Director*. Lexington, Kentucky : University Press of Kentucky, [2013], 2013.

Warshow, Robert. "The Gangster as Tragic Hero." 1948. *The Immediate Experience: Movies, Comics, Theatre and Other Aspects of Popular Culture*. Cambridge: Harvard U Press, 2001. 97–104. Print.

Warshow, Robert. "Movie Chronicle: The Westerner." 1954. *The Immediate Experience: Movies, Comics, Theatre and Other Aspects of Popular Culture*. Cambridge: Harvard U Press, 2001. 105–24. Print.

The Westerner. Dir. William Wyler. Perf. Gary Cooper, Walter Brennan. United Artists Corp., 1940. DVD.

Andrew Rahman

Ambisonics, or 360° sound, is a surround sound audio technology that incorporates the vertical axis in addition to the horizontal. It has been around since the 1970's but due to the space and processing power required it never established itself in the consumer market. Now, thanks to the abundance of powerful personal computers, ambisonics is making a resurgence. In this project I explore recording in ambisonics using a soundfield microphone by capturing impulse responses, or sonic snapshots, of acoustically and historically interesting buildings. These recordings are used in convolution reverb, a software audio effect which, when audio is run through, simulates that audio playing in the recorded building. With ambisonics, the addition of the vertical axis allows sounds to be virtually be placed anywhere in the room, including above and below the listener. While ambisonics is currently used predominately in virtual reality, it has the potential to expand into education, film, and music. Until recently this technology has been inaccessible to consumers and there are few definitive introductory resources. This paper serves as a gateway into ambisonics for consumers, audiophiles, composers, film makers, video game designers, and early adopters.

Andrew Rahman
B.A. Music, 2017

Faculty Mentor: Edmund Campion, Music

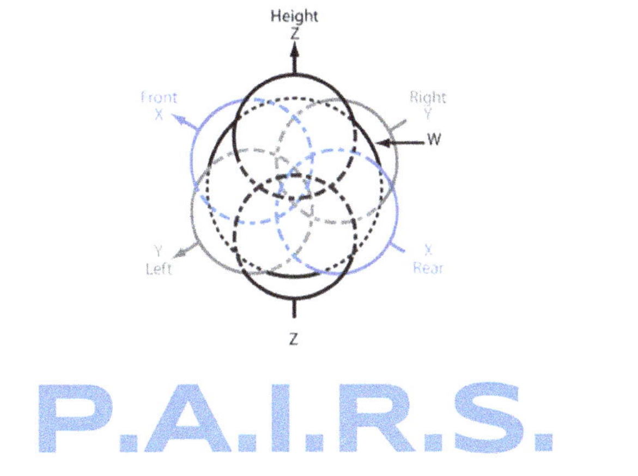

Portable Ambisonic Impulse Response System

An Introduction to Ambisonic Impulse Response Recording

Andrew Rahman

Andrew Rahman, *P.A.I.R.S.*, 2016–2017. Portable ambisonic impulse response system, recorded ambisonic impulse responses, research paper. 24.6 x 19.7 x 14.4 inches/12:28 minutes.

PUBLIC WORKS

BISHAL DUTTA
IAN SHEERIN
CECELIA DIMINO
THE RENEGADE CLASSROOM
ZHIFEI XU
AURORE DEVELAY
ABOUBACAR KOMARA
JAMES PAYNE

Bishal Dutta

"The 9 to 5" is a short documentary about an undocumented filmmaker in Los Angeles traversing his surroundings—his neighborhood, the mall at which he works, a film set—in order to come to terms with the ugliness and beauty of his world. It began as a small documentary prompt for a class at UC Berkeley but grew into something much more significant and timely. My primary collaborator, Gabriel Santos, and I discussed ways in which we could subvert the traditional, "feel-good" social documentary. It was only upon the discovery of our subject, who will remain anonymous, that we found ourselves in the eye of the storm that is the political discourse around undocumented immigrants.

Our goal was to capture a truthful portrait of an extraordinary individual while also allowing his voice to blossom as a mouthpiece for a repressed collective voice. As filmmakers, our greatest resource for understanding our subject's hopes and dreams was our own passion for cinema, one that he shares. We settled on shooting without traditional interviews, instead walking through real streets, discussing, understanding, disagreeing, and synthesizing our own conclusions on what it is to be undocumented.

Bishal Dutta
B.A. Film and Media Studies, 2018

Faculty Mentor: Linda Williams, Film & Media

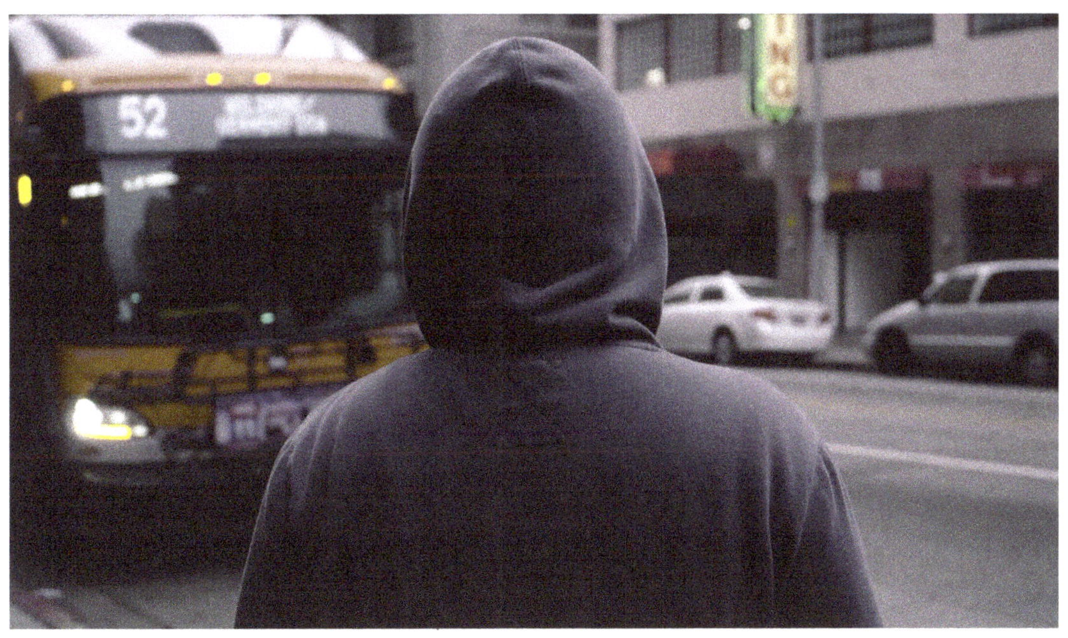

Bishal Dutta, *The 9 to 5*, 2017. Color, digital video, 4:27 minutes.

Ian Sheerin

The cracks that thread through our society often appear the most pronounced at its margins. At the heart of 'Street Beggar' is an attempt to give voice to the recognition of shared plight; it's also a breath of air and light into the all-too-isolated, and shadowy blind spot of American consumer culture; it's poor and forgotten who are, in a way, all of us. By highlighting what beauty remains in the eyes of the thoroughly beaten, sad casualties of a culture of distraction and instant gratification, there is an oblique criticism of value which challenges where and how beauty and meaning are sought and discovered.

Ian Sheerin
B.A. English, 2018
Ina Coolbrith Memorial Poetry Prize, 2017

Faculty Mentor: Eric Falci, English

Street Beggar

The man came in tatters
you averted your eyes
I saw the way you looked down
suddenly so taken
with the ground
But as he passes you in the street
he catches your eye
and within that turmoil
sweating, tanned, alive
the cosmos of his face
appears suddenly somehow
sweet
Absolved
by a crinkle of his eye
the memory of a smile
wind blowing the curtains
sunlight through the backdoor
The shuffling saint owns naught
but the broken mirror he holds
Oh, my love
It is without price

Cecelia DiMino

Chords for Progression *provides a unique way for newcomer refugee/asylum-seeking high school youth with a history of interrupted schooling to "catch-up." In Oakland Unified School District, there has been a 122% increase in the number of newcomers over the past two years. At Castlemont High School, at least 50% of the 250 newcomers are Students with Limited or Interrupted Formal Education, coming from countries where poverty, disaster, civil unrest, and/or persecution have affected their development of literacy and opportunities for education. Many are fleeing violence and human trafficking.* Chords for Progression *will be approaching their intensive academic and socio-emotional needs through an after-school program that merges math with musicianship and dance, while also facilitating English language learning. The music program utilizes the Orff-Schulwerk Method composed of barred instruments and percussion; the math program follows K-6 Common Core Standards. Program features include: geometry via dance and the visual arts; algebra via acting; fractions and graphing via hip-hop. Students will be thinking, doing, touching, creating, playing in math and music. This program is anticipated to amplify academic and language capability, self-esteem, confidence, and also promote emotional healing; higher attendance rates, less tardiness, better grades and an overall more successful schooling experience is expected.*

Cecelia DiMino
B.A. Linguistics, 2018
Big Ideas Winner & Strauss Foundation Award, 2017

Faculty Mentor: Phillip Denny, Blum Center for Developing Economies

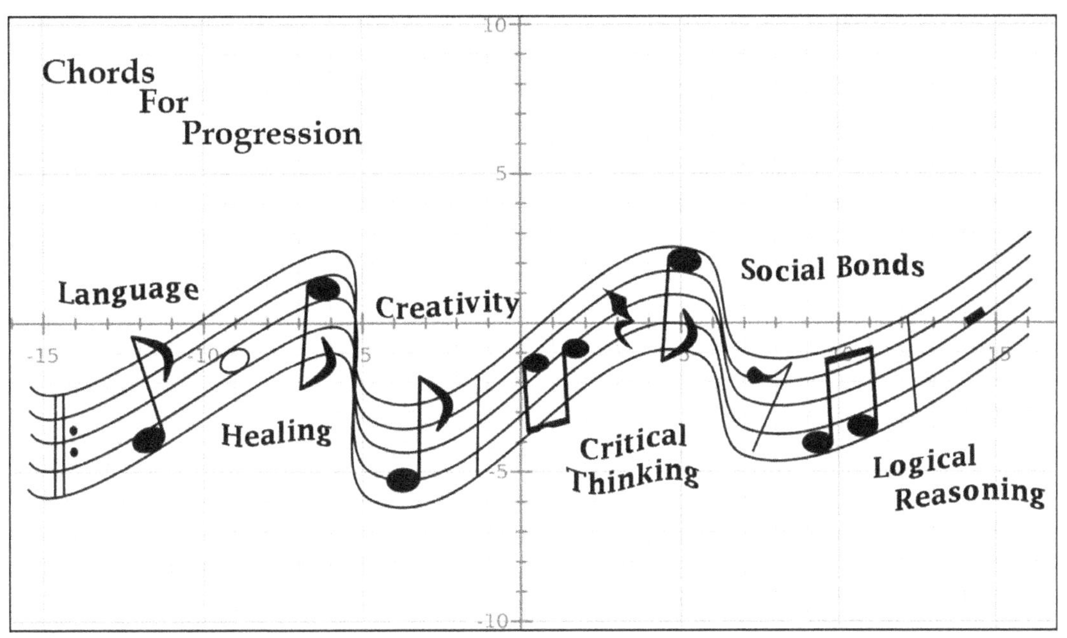

Cecelia DiMino, *Chords for Progression*, 2017. After school program,
3 days per week, 3 hours per day, 27 weeks in total.

The Renegade Classroom

The Renegade Classroom is a multi-benefit public structure designed to address the unique needs of REALM Charter High School and the surrounding West Berkeley community. The design came out of conversations with REALM students, teachers, and leadership, as well as a variety of external experts and community members. Set on George Florence Park, the Renegade Classroom will serve as an educational space for REALM and a public amenity for the wider community. The classroom is sited within a public park in response to REALM's lack of educational space on their own campus and their desire for more engaging learning environments. This proposed site also enables the classroom to activate an underutilized park and address the surrounding community's limited access to beautiful public facilities.

The classroom is comprised of two parts: an instructional space with amphitheater seating and a large, flexible lab space configured with stow-away tables. With the ability to introduce lessons in the instructional space and then move on to the open air lab, this combination is a fitting facilitator of REALM's project-based learning curriculum. For the community, the space is an ideal environment to host events such as public meetings, concerts, outdoor movie screenings, and private parties.

Ryan Alexander
B.A. Sustainable Environmental Design, 2017

Lila Frisher
B.A. Sustainable Environmental Design,
Minor in City and Regional Planning, 2017

Can Ceyhan
B.A. Sustainable Environmental Design,
Minor in GIS and Political Economy, 2017

Jeff Schaefer
B.A. Sustainable Environmental Design,
Minor in GIS, 2017

Oriya Cohen
B.A. Sustainable Environmental Design,
Minor in City and Regional Planning, 2017

Faculty Mentor: Emily Pilloton, College of Environmental Design

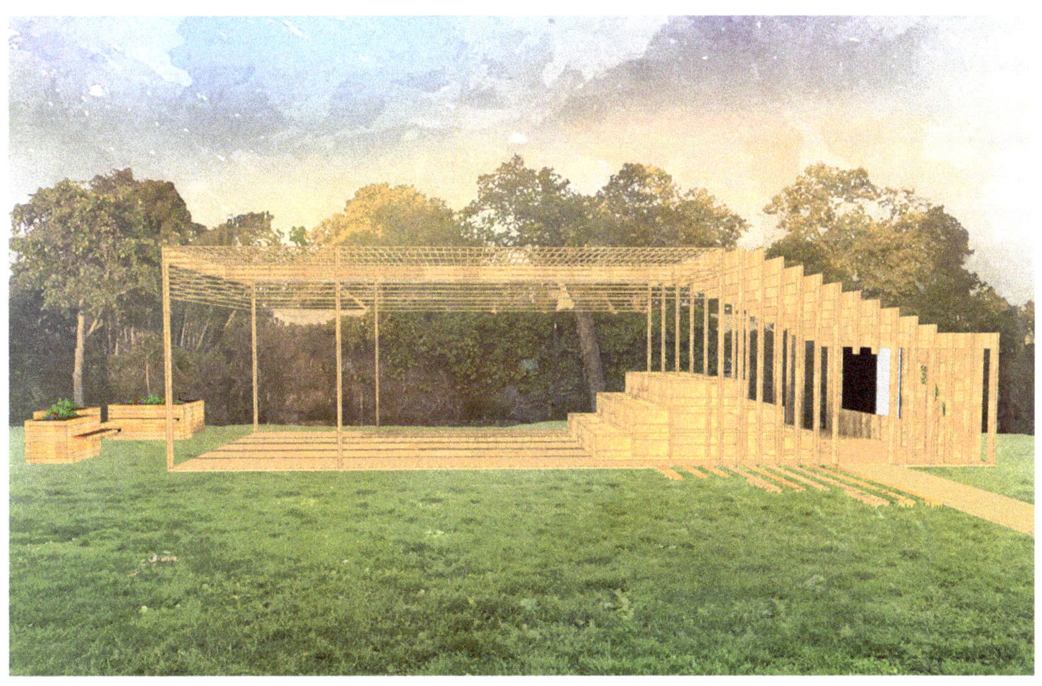

Ryan Alexander, Can Ceyhan, Oriya Cohen, Lila Frisher, Jeff Schaefer, *The Renegade Classroom*, 2017. Digital design, 16 x 10 feet.

Zhifei Xu

The site is located in an abandoned quarry in Rockridge, Oakland, and I intend to explore a poetic alternative to the current careless abandonment of quarries in Oakland. The project incorporates a Planetarium and a Geological Exploratorium and captures Genius loci, celebrating the timeless quality of the stone, sky, and water, while it re-links surrounding urban fabrics that are currently disconnected.

The project's primary geometry in the plan resembles the orbiting of the planets and the order of the universe, echoing the theme of timelessness. In the section, the geometry is deconstructed in order to fit the local geological condition and celebrate the fact of the transience of the building itself.

This project accepts the constructed nature and it humbly submerges its monumentality underneath the water, only giving a few hints by the popping out skylights. It quietly waits underneath the surface like a silent stone, for the visitors to come through the cycle and explore the deep sensation in the heart intrigued by the light and space and the timelessness of the content.

Zhifei Xu
B.A. Architecture, 2017
Circus Student Winner, 2017

Faculty Mentor: Rene Davids, College of Environmental Design

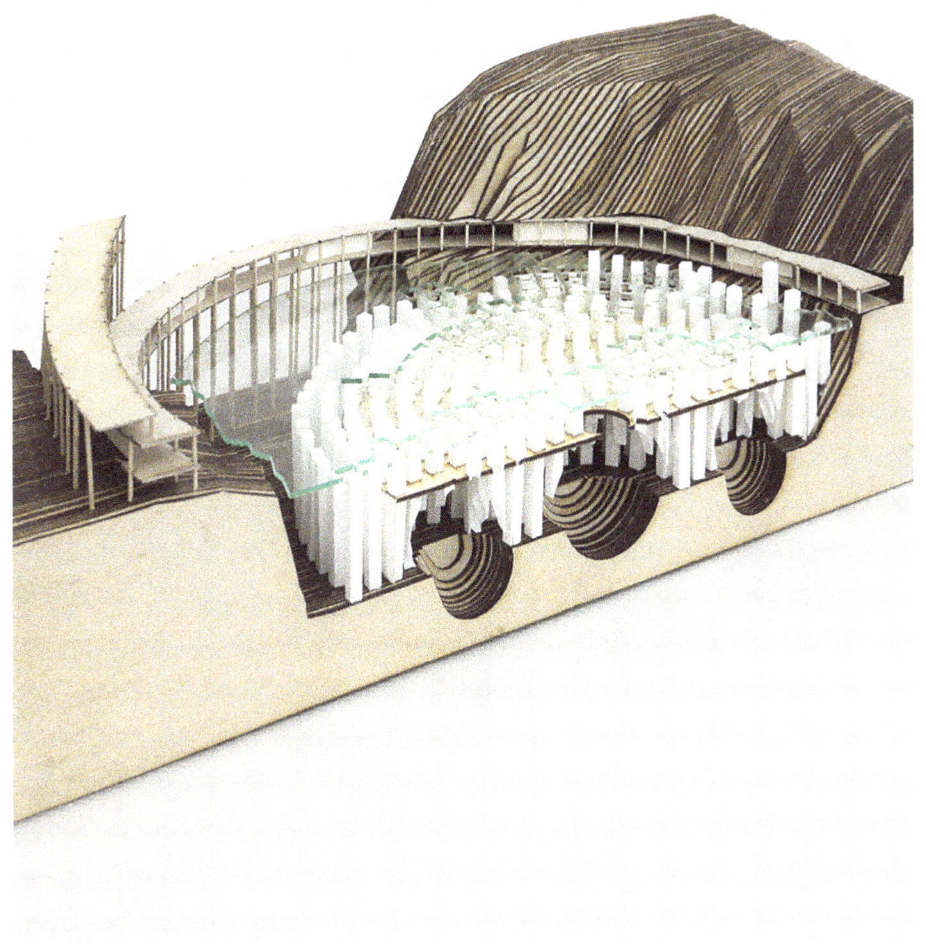

Zhifei Xu, *Timeless Celebration,* 2016. Digital, print on paper, wood, dimensions variable.

Aurore Develay

The Bay Bridge Trail takes place at a major transition point, not only between highways, but also between land and water, as well as yesterday and tomorrow, both culturally and historically. The site, previously home of indigenous tribes, is now populated with invasive, non-native plant species.

Originally designed as a satirical response, the Underpass Native Garden is a botanical garden that is exclusively composed of plant species native to the San Francisco Bay.

A series of oversized diamond-shaped planters, whose aggressive form may be perceived as an allusion to Native American arrowheads, creates an intriguing pattern which can be visited at two scales and speeds, by both pedestrians (on the ground) and drivers (on the highway overpass). The Underpass Native Garden constitutes the reverse invasion of native species.

The south-east facing planters, held by concrete walls of varying heights, protect the plants from strong winds while producing an interesting interaction between the visitors and the gigantic Star-Wars-like elements. The Underpass Native Garden, whose pattern could be used as a template for further development along the trail or for other LAEP projects, is part of a new generation of botanical gardens, which stand for ecological sustainability.

Aurore Develay
B.A. Landscape Architecture and Environmental Planning, 2018
Circus Student Winner, 2017

Faculty Mentor: Jennifer Brooks, College of Environmental Design

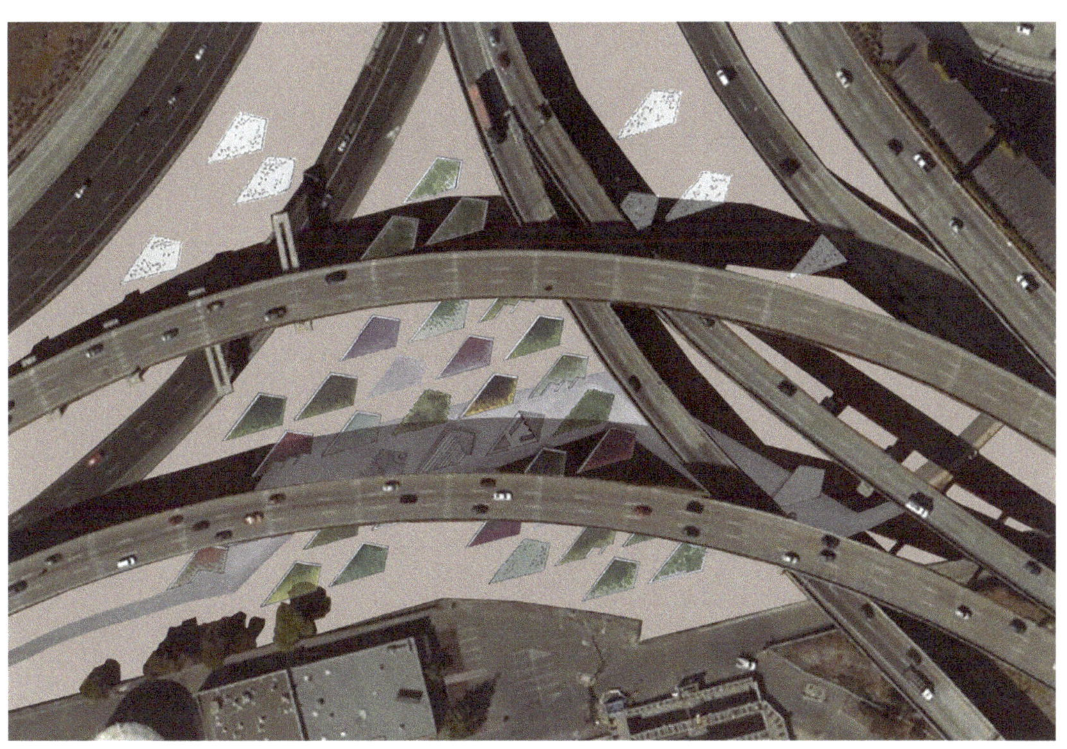

Aurore Develay, *Underpass Native Garden*, 2016. Drawings, plans, models, photomontages, dimensions variable.

Aboubacar Komara

The Potrero library project consisted of the design of a library in San Francisco. The class exercise started with the exploration of the Double Negative concept, which consisted of having at least two voids intercepting in a solid volume to create the Double Negative spaces. As I moved forward through the design of this library, I was interested in the concept of Design for Health and Design for Engagement, which later had major impacts on the project.

To promote walking long distances in the library, the circulation consisted of voids going through the diagonal of the library, the longest length possible on the site. These diagonal voids sheltered the principal stair around which all the bookshelves are arranged. Having diagonal circulations also allowed the creation of triangular program spaces that have a unique effect on the users' experiences. The bookshelves were designed to serve as a key element in this library. In addition to their primary function as bookshelves, they served as structural elements to support the building and, finally, they also served to control the amount of lighting that enters the different spaces. In conclusion, through these concepts I was able to design a library that solved recent issues while preventing future problems.

Aboubacar Komara
B.A. Architecture, 2018
Circus Student Winner, 2017

Faculty Mentor: Juliana Raimondi, College of Environmental Design

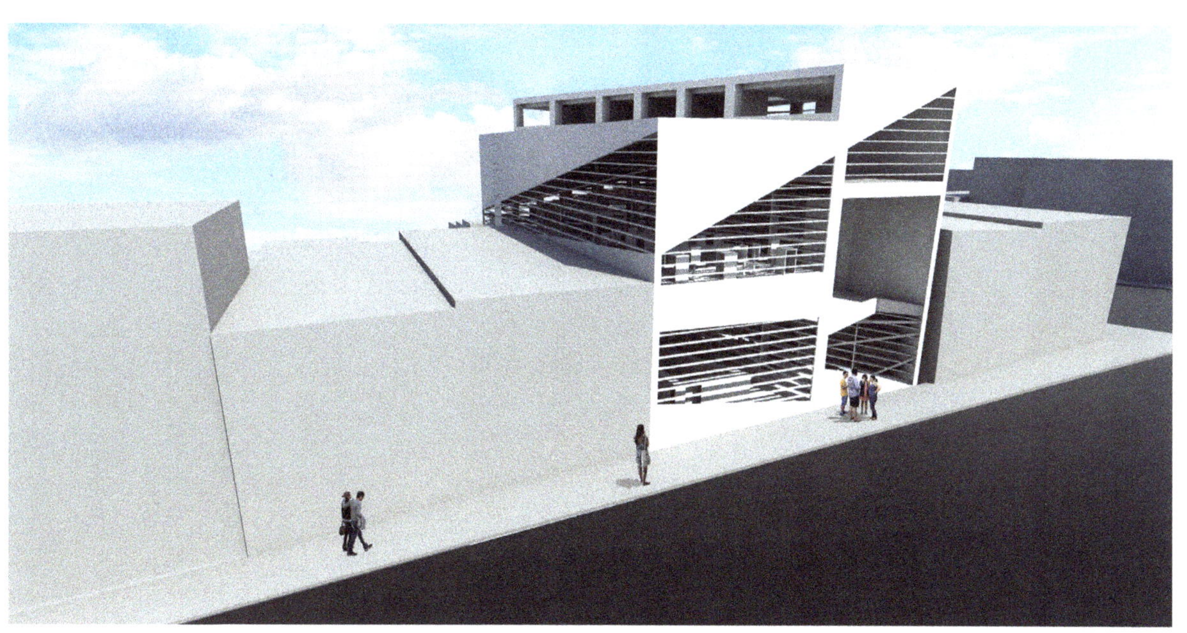

Aboubacar Komara, *Potrero Hill Library*, 2016. Digital design, dimensions variable.

James Payne

This poem is a snap shot of how my mind would quickly digress as I sat at my desk that looks over the neighborhood Ghost Town in Oakland where I lived during my time at Cal. From my small dark room I felt like a fly on the wall and also trapped. I fed off of the culture that downtown Oakland provided but I also like I was the brunt of a housing shortage.

James Payne
B.A. English, Minor in History and Creative Writing, 2017
Ina Coolbrith Memorial Poetry Prize, 2017

Faculty Mentors: John Shoptaw, Geoffrey O'Brien, Robert Hass, English

Ghost Town

There was one time that I had no choice, I was born in 1984,
the same year Grove was renamed MLK Way. Stuttered shots,
I turned a lamp off and the window framed late grey. Cavities
nestled a condemned state building, a Buick on 29th was left
crooked and running. The lights were on, the driver had left a
door open like something terrible had happened, or had been.

Shrunken cars flew on an on-ramp through the trees on 30th,
vanished behind chipping homes they might've been crashing
into the grid of numbers and civil rights figures, but were just
frantic from the rushed demise of hours and warm pot roast.
To their cul de sacs, named after birds and revolutionaries, forgotten lawn and touch up jobs, I'd never written in a dark grey.

FRIENDS AND STRANGERS

Bennett Shaeffer

Through "untitled," I intended to tackle the issue of isolation in a room full of like-minded people. Anyone who knows me can attest to my love of going to arts and culture shows alone, as I feel that everyone in the room is a potential new friend who can shape and inspire my future. After all, everyone there has at least one thing in common—the fact that they are all together for the same event. Sadly, this optimism is sometimes overly ambitious, as many people would rather spend time with their current friends instead of taking a leap into the unfamiliar. Through this installation, I intend to strip that mindset by encouraging friend groups to split apart and mingle with those they do not know. As new groups are formed, the audio/visuals also grows, generatively feeding off the love of strangers. If the normal bonds of social interaction stand, however, the music and visuals will become stale and eerie, directing the room to try a new configuration.

Bennett Shaeffer
B.A Undeclared, 2019

Faculty Mentors: Rama Gottfried, Music

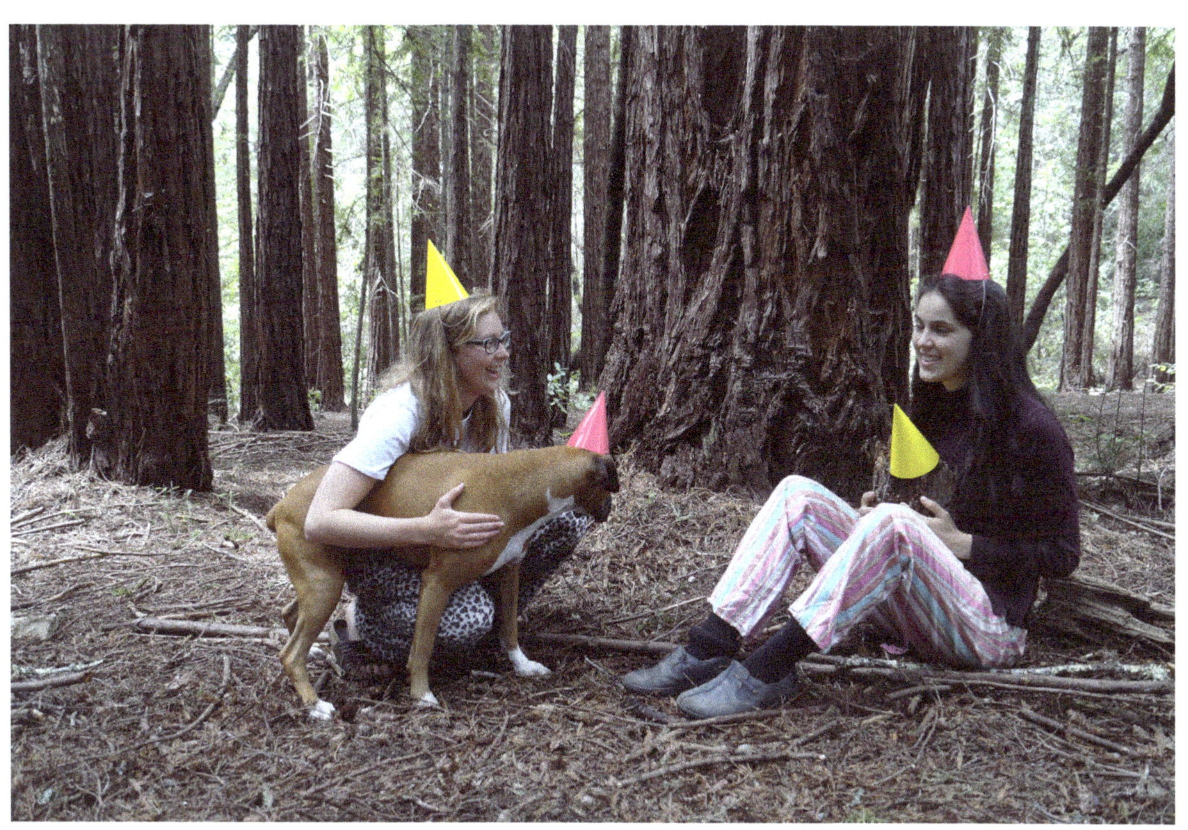

Bennett Shaeffer, *untitled*, 2017. Performance piece.

Paige Davis and Weston Smith

The work, made up of twelve pieces by each of us, is a dialogue and a quiet interview with most of what was made and said, left unseen. It is a work of listening and playing, then of daily life examined and separated, and dailiness, nothing but the passage of time. Together as co-authors, co-ordinators, we've made some form of writing and cataloguing.

Paige Davis
B.A. Art Practice and American Studies, 2017
Honors Program Awardee, Fall 2016
and Departmental Citation (Art Practice)

Weston Smith
B.A. Art Practice, 2017
Honors Program Awardee, Fall 2016
and Wendy Sussman Memorial Award in Painting, 2017

Faculty Mentor: Allan deSouza, Art Practice

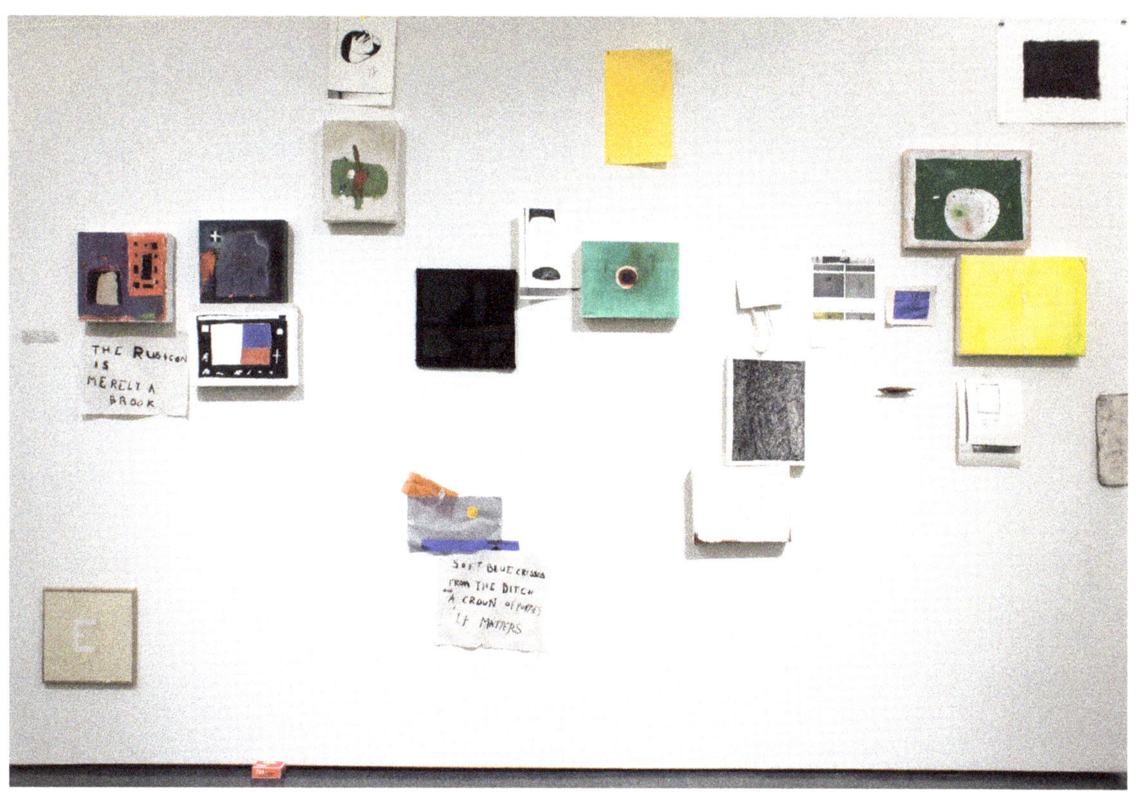

Paige Davis and Weston Smith, *Over Alls (Field Report)*, 2016–2017. Oil on canvas, oil on birch panel, oil on newsprint with crayon and pencil, oil on paper, oil on linen, ink jet prints, grandparents' nylon ripstop, marker on paper, embroidery thread, found photo, felt, hair, found box, gifted canvas, ink on paper, pencil on paper, oil on iron with masking tape and wire, manzanita from Mt. Tamalpais with olive oil from Stoupa, 24 objects. Dimensions variable.

Shrinking Violets

Background "Shrinking Violets" comes from an old idiom, which refers to shy individuals. Much like a "Wallflower," Shrinking Violets appear shy and often have trouble overcoming their fears. This project came to be after five shy individuals wanted to come up with a unique way to challenge the human condition of shyness; we were inspired by the strange robot, Shybot, which avoided human contact by roaming locations attempting to seek solitude. This led us to question how in the modern, interconnectedness of our lives, we can help promote self-happiness & appreciate the human condition of being shy.

Kate Masancay
B.A. Media Studies, 2017

Sharon Wang
B.A. Media Studies, 2018

Sebastian Ospina
B.A. Cognitive Science, 2017

Peggy Zhao
B.A. Cognitive Science, 2017

Shota Pangilinan
B.A. Cognitive Science, 2017

Faculty Mentor: Sara Beckman, Haas School of Business

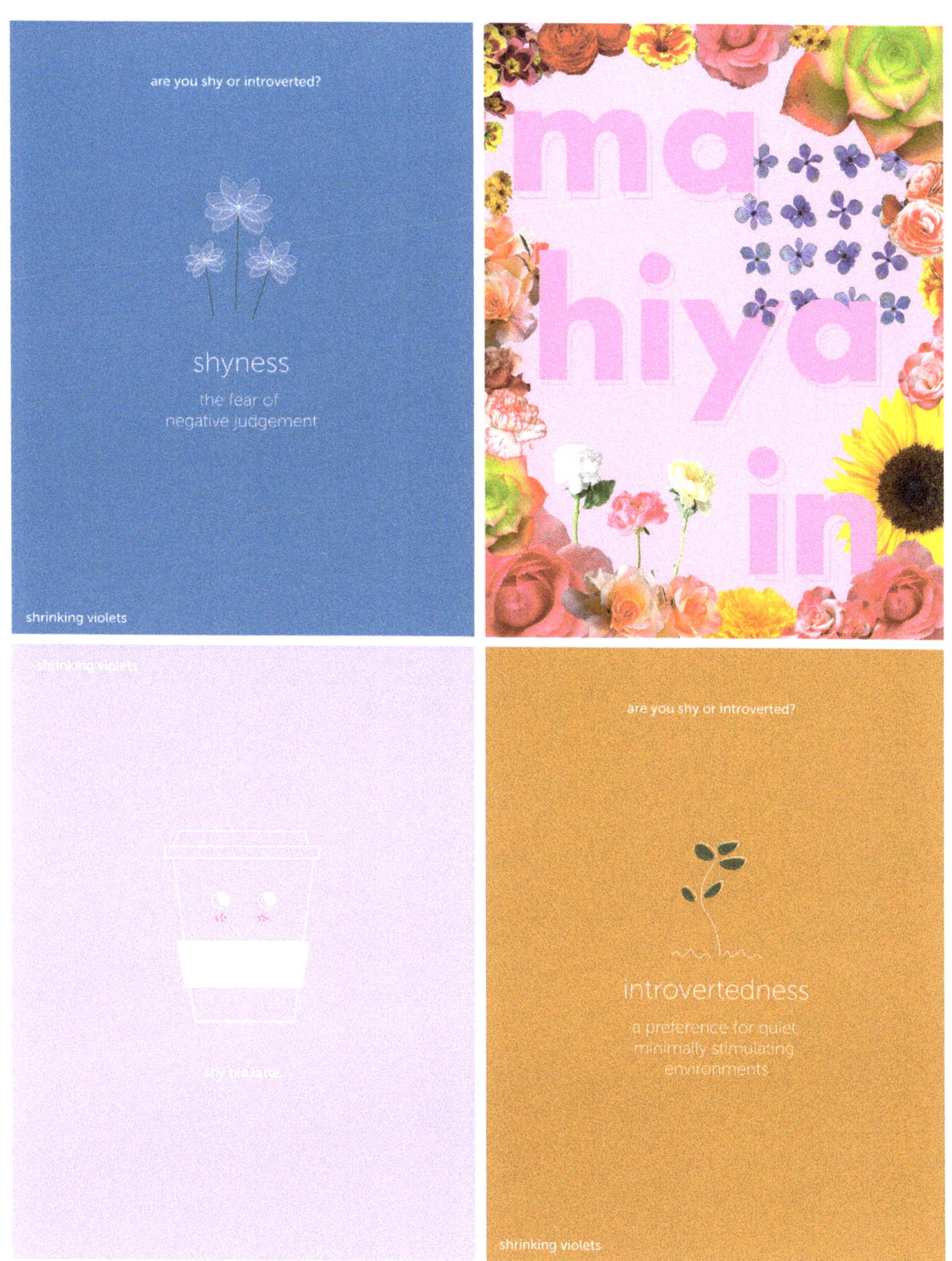

Kate Masancay, Sebastian Ospina, Shota Pangilinan, Sharon Wang, Peggy Zhao, *Shrinking Violets*, 2017. Digital illustration, iOS prototyping, and ¼ acrylic lasercut, dimensions variable.

Kyler Ernst

A visual artist reaches out to an old friend through Facebook to request a particular "inappropriate" image of the artist's work be taken down. When it is revealed that the friend has been diagnosed with a serious illness, the artist is forced to decide between letting the request go or to continue pressing, friendship and reputation be damned... the artist doesn't choose wisely.

Kyler Ernst
B.A. English, 2018
The Yoshiko Uchida Prize for Fiction, 2017

Faculty Mentors: Namwali Serpell, English

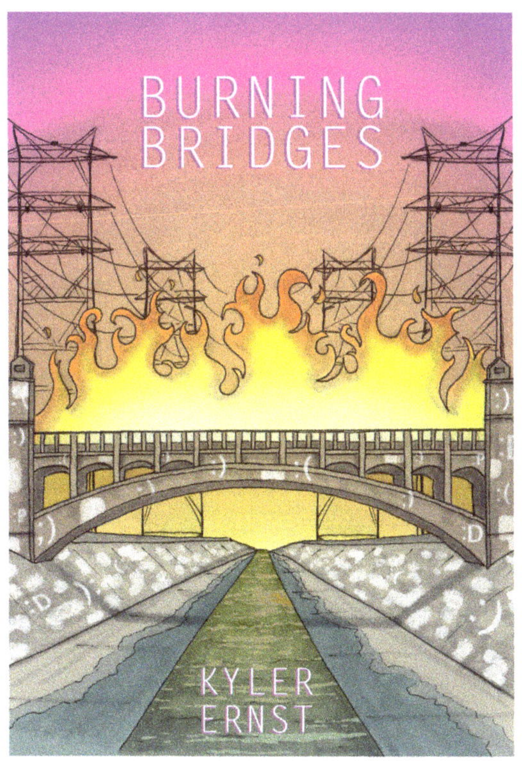

12/12/2016 7:11PM

Morgan! How are you? How's the family? I truly hope you're doing well. Regretfully, I have a small favor to ask of you. There is a picture on your profile that I would very much appreciate if you could take down. It's from when you came here to LA a couple years ago (for a work conference, I believe?) and you graciously visited my studio. Remember you took a few pictures with the two of us? To be clear, it's not a problem at all that you posted them because I remember that for various reasons I okayed us taking pictures in the first place and also consented to the specific photos that you posted to facebook at the time, but my professional situation has changed since then (in a good way!) which now makes one in particular inappropriate to share. Here it is: [link] Specifically, the background of the photo in question reveals a part of my process that wasn't too integral to my practice at the time but has since become a major element of my most current and successful work, and I'd prefer to keep it private. And since I found the photo through an online search of my name, others could find it too! So you would be doing me a HUGE favor if you could remove the photo as soon as it is convenient—I'm sure you've got your hands full with the kids! Thank you, Morgan, and I sincerely hope you're doing superb!

12/18/2016 9:32PM

Morgan, it's been almost a week and I'm not sure you've seen my message. Is facebook the best way to reach you? I can't find you anywhere else online and unfortunately I can't find your number on my phone (my phone is ancient!). I only have your old USC email and I'm sure you don't use it, but I copy/pasted the earlier message and emailed it to you anyway. (Just to be safe, I'll be emailing you in addition to these messages until I've heard back from you.) Since I've had some time to think about it, I feel I should try to explain my situation a bit better. I sincerely do not want to oend you about the photo because it's 100% not a personal issue at all. I'm not sure if you've been seeing my more recent updates (are you on instagram?), but things have finally started to take o for me. I've had seven shows (!) in the past 11 months and I have my very first solo show at Shulamit Nazarian that opens next March. The show is called "Tracing the Void: Illusions of Presence." It will feature similar kind of installation pieces that you saw in my studio, but much more ambitious. I'm pretty sure I've explained to you Kanizsa's Triangle? How the illusion of a triangle is achieved through the strategic placement of shapes and fragments to make the mind assume the presence rather than the absence of form? (Of course this is just to give you an idea: my work as you know is much more complex.) To put it simply, my work attempts to negotiate the relationship between "presence" and "absence" by engendering an ambivalent semantic structure of meaning through the deliberate use of aesthetically and ethically challenging optical eects. Ahh! I'm sure I've told you this a million times! Sorry! I know that ever since you moved away and started a family you haven't been making as much art as you used to, but I trust you understand why removing the photo is so important. I won't insult you by explaining it!

12/18/2016 9:40PM

It's just that my artistic practice hinges on this process, and if my process becomes public knowledge, it potentially devalues the work.

12/18/2016 9:40PM

But I should add that you should totally feel free to keep the rest of the photos online from that day, as none of those reveal anything important. :)

12/25/2016 3:18PM

Merry Christmas!!! I saw you just posted a photo with the family—the matching red sweaters are very endearing! Bozeman looks like a winter wonderland. I'm enjoying the holidays here in lala land. (Couldn't get away to see family this year—way too busy prepping for my show!) It's even warmer than usual this time of year, and since every apartment in Boyle Heights doubles as a convection oven, I'm wearing shorts and sandals today. Wanna trade places? :P In all seriousness, it looks like we're both enjoying the holidays. I'm drinking spiked eggnog and my roommate just put some xmas lights on the agave plant in the kitchen, so now I just need you to send me some of that cooler weather! You can keep the snow! ;) Hope you're well!

✓ Seen 3:22PM

12/25/2016 3:23PM

Heyyy! How are you??

01/01/2016 12:03AM

happy new year! you still up?

01/08/2016 10:02AM

Morgan, I just read your heartbreaking update. I'm at a loss for words! I want to tell you how terribly sorry I am to hear about your diagnosis. Obviously I had no idea that this was something you were dealing with. It's very clear you have a big community of support, and your family will be there with you every step of the way. And of course all of us from afar will be there for you as well—including me. I wish you the best of luck with your ongoing tests and treatment. Take care of yourself, and please know that I am keeping you in my thoughts.

01/012/2016 9:21AM

Morgan, I saw your post about the fundraising campaign. You've already raised a quarter of your goal—that's incredible! As you very aptly said in the campaign description, it's truly alarming how steep medical costs can be, even with company insurance, but the fact that you can share this and get so much support in such a short amount of time truly speaks volumes. I still work the front desk at the dentist oce downtown (walking distance to my studio) and most of my extra funds goes toward paying studio rent, but I promise after my next paycheck to donate as much as I can—but I'm 100% confident that you're going to raise the money you need! Take care and get well soon!

01/17/2017 8:33PM

Morgan, I read your latest post about your recovery, and I think you're very brave to be so open about the entire process—it must be very dicult and you have my utmost respect. Let me know if there's anything I can do to help. I'm keeping you in my thoughts!

02/01/2017 11:02AM

Morgan, I want to apologize if I oended you with my earlier messages about the photo. If I had known about your diagnosis, I would never have contacted you the way that I did. You absolutely should be focusing on your health and your loved ones right now. So I really do feel genuinely terrible to ask again if you could take the photo down whenever you can. I'm sure that you've got a lot on your mind right now, so maybe if you'd be willing to give me your password to log into your account I could delete the photo for you and then you could change the password afterwards? Would this be possible? Of course I'm 100% open to suggestions...

02/08/2017 2:56PM

Morgan, I think I may have overstepped in my last message. I sincerely apologize. There are absolutely sno excuses for the tone of that message—I wrote it while I was at work and I was distracted with a number of phone calls as I was composing it and also I've been very tired after consecutive late nights in the studio. But I want you to know that you have been in my thoughts every day since the diagnosis and I respect your situation 100%. So please know that I'm fully aware of how this must sound under the circumstances, but the photo has serious implications for my career. It may be hard for you to understand since you gave up on the artist thing years ago, but I'm sure that you at least partially get where I'm coming from? My professional ambitions probably pale in comparison to the life you've made for yourself in Montana, but it would help if tried to see it from my perspective.

02/08/2017 2:57PM

Please read what i just wrote in the sincerest way possible..! .you truly deserve all thats happened toyou since leaving grad school. .!

02/08/2017 2:57PM

i mean other than the diangoniss..let me know if there's anything i can do to help...

02/08/2017 2:57PM

*diagnosis

02/08/2017 7:19PM

Morgan, I'm sorry. I wrote that last message while at work again. I just left Dr. Beck's oce and I'm finally writing without any distractions—I'm at my studio and my studio neighbor lent me her headphones. I really feel like my recent words may have put a strain on our friendship but I'm being 100% honest when I say that you were one of my best friends in grad school. Do you remember how we used to get french fries at the restaurant across the street? I don't remember what it was called, but we used to sit together—this was before I stopped painting—and have "painter confessions". Remember that? We only did it three or four times and we didn't really see each other much after that (other than that one walk we took) but I'm being 100% honest when I say that those painter confessions were a major reason I made it through my first year. When you dropped out that summer and moved back home, I truly didn't know who I was going to talk to! I was really hoping we were going to stay friends. Not that we're not friends now! You should know that you're welcome to come visit me whenever you want to...or you can save the plane ticket and just message me back. ;)

02/08/2017 11:42PM

hi.. .still at the stuido..somtimes my hands shake so mch i cant make anything.has that ever happened to you.? when u paint do yur hands ever shake.? do you still paint? there is still so much to do before the show.. i dnt know how im gong to do all ofit.. sorry for the bad typing im on my phone the battery on my computer died and i left my charger at my apt. sory for the emotional crap.. ill be fine!!. just another late nite

02/14/2017 10:02AM

At work again. Hope you're having a better a Valentine's day than I am. everything smells like plaque and the phones won't stop ringing. So Dr. beck told me a joke yesterday that dental patients can't keep their mouths shut but getting them to talk is like pulling teeth... so last night i dreamt that there were rooms of people with their mouths open and dr. beck was using surgical instruments to extract words from their heads. weird huh?

02/15/2017 7:03PM

Hey, just got back to the studio and saw the video you posted. You're painting again! The self-portrait is beautiful—you are still a master with colors. :D I'm genuinely sorry to hear about the pain but just know you truly look incredible under the circumstances. Are you sure you're sick? ;)

✓ Seen 11:23PM

02/15/2017 11:24PM

Hello?

02/15/2017 11:25PM

Morgan?

02/28/2017 9:03PM

Hi, Moran. How are you. I was just at Brian Gonzalez's opening at The Pit and I talked with him for a couple minutes and here's what he said to me verbatim: I think I figured out how you make those trippy optical illusions. You and Brian are friends, right? I'm not accusing you of telling him anything, but maybe because of everything that's been happening with you he was looking through old photos on facebook and saw the one I've been trying to tell you about? Or maybe he randomly googled my name and saw it pop up on the search results just like I did? I don't want to burn any bridges but I think that maybe you should have paid a little more attention to what I have been asking you instead of ignoring my messages. I know that I sound like the worst person in the world to say this to someone who is sick but I don't know what I'm supposed to do in this situation. If Brian tells other people about it then everyone else will start searching for it too and that's the last thing I need. I just need to survive until my show before anyone else finds out but the only way that can happen is if you please please please read this message and help me out! This probably sounds more desperate than I actually feel...just been a long week!

02/28/2017 9:04PM

*Morgan

03/01/2017 12:19AM

i went strait to the studio after brian;s show.. im still here . working. i wonder if anyone truly gets what im trying to do with my work..maybe if you understood you would try to help me. the whole thing is you cant have presence without absence and you cant have absence without presence and thats what this is all about you know? we see a triangle because in the end we really want one to be there. and we cant unsee it even after we understand the illusion. the more we try to unsee it the more clear it becomes. like me for instance. im not with you right now but there are enough parts of me to give the illusion that im totally here you know? you can't see my face or my skin or my hair or my eyebrows or my lips so how are you sure im here? but you know 100% that im here despite everything thats missing and you might not knowit but you want me to be here andthats what makes it more real than anything. im just using me as an example it could be anyone.. but seriusly why wont you talk to me?. please forgive me okay? sory im a little drunk.. .have a goodnight

03/08/2017 1:32AM

Morgan, oh no no no! How could they misdiagnose??? If they were wrong about that how can you trust them when they say you only have a few weeks?? How could that happen???? Oh I'm so sorry morgan im so so sorry remember that we all love you very much

03/10/2017 4:55PM

So I did some research and there are more options out there. Have you looked into a naturopathic treatment? There are almost fifty certified naturopathic doctors within three hundred miles of you, and I found the best one: [link] Her name is Dr. Priya Singh and she's based in Spokane, WA. Her patient reviews are five stars across the board and she treats even the most extreme cases. I even looked at her schedule and she is accepting new patients as early as two weeks from now but if you call her and tell her your situation maybe she'll make an exception. Don't give up hope.

03/19/2017 2:56AM

I'm sorry, I can't read your blog posts anymore. Frankly, you share too much and I find it oensive. Do you ever wonder what that does to a person to hear so many emotional things?don't you ever worry that it might be burdening the other person? Haven't you ever wondered if your the one whois being selfish? you get to share and reveal everything that you feel like revealing and then you get to ignore everything I'm telling you..yuu know what I dont care how this might sound to you Its bullshit that you think your better than me just because you walked away and i didnt. I stuck it out and took my bruises and now im finally making it work for me out here and if chasing the thing I care about the most is a waste of a life then im glad im fucking wasting it. Ill waste it so hard that there will be nothing left when im gone. .everything i touch will go down with me.. no kids no family no friends no life.. how does that sound?. is that what youu exptected? did you expect some sort of apology when you dropped out and updated everyone with thatstupid facebook post? whenyou said "i dropped out. peace art peeps". I hate myself that i remember it exactly and I hate myself even more that im so positive that i remembered it exactly.. did you think we al cried and waved our white flags when you left.?? do youu?? well we didnt sogo fuck yourself

03/19/2017 2:57AM

im sorry im scard out of mind about my show and all of this is srlsy too much for me to handle rightnow pleasse dont think this is how i really feeel ..this is jsut my emotinos tlking

03/19/2017 2:57AM

*emotions

03/19/2017 11:41AM

Morgan, I wanted to notify you that I reported the photo to Facebook. I have made sure not to implicate you in my report, but I did label it as inappropriate and harmful to my public and professional image. This should not have any repercussions for you. I sincerely apologize that it had to be taken this far and I wish you all the best.—Sam

03/29/2017 11:56PM

everyone is posting on your wall but i know the truth. i know youre not gone because nothing feels dierent. nothing feels dierent at all and something would have changed if you were really gone. i would have felt it i know it. it would be really nice if youd say hello.

03/30/2017 2:03AM

hello?

03/30/2017 4:41AM

hello

03/31/2017 8:18PM

hey...im at my opening.. so muchhas happened!! i just had totell someone about it.. sooo many poeple came.. everone keeps teling methat im giong to be huuge after this which istoo mcuh to even proces rightnow.. .im hiding in the bathroom .people keep knockig but im not redy to come out yet..my hands keep shaking..its ben a wierd night.. dont you hate it that evryone at art openings look at yur forhead when you talk tothem??? it makesme feel like theyare trying to read my thoughts..its realy weird to be theonly artist in the show..all eyes areon me..thers an art collector that im dead seriuos is wearing a shiny purpl suit who keeps asking me if my work was made with assitnts or if i made it al with my own hands..i just told him i had to goto the bathroom...but it rly is going insnely well..it just feels a litle wierd you kno.w.? its hardto describe how i feell..i mean wut is the bigest moment in yur life supposd to feel like.? do you remembr when we wnt tothe bridge? we walked overa mile to get there.. and i was talking about something but after awhile i realized that you werent really listening..or you were just being really quiet and i couldnt tell if you were listening..and so i finally stopped talking when we got to the bridge and we just stood there..and both of us didnt say anything .we just stood there and were quiet and we looked at the la river trickling through the concrete below us..passing beneath us on the bridge..and for the longest time we were just perfectly quiet..just breathing.. and then after a very long time you sighed and you said..well wasnt that nice? and it was. it was really really really nice.

Amanda

Welcome to Amanda, your new social media assistant! Amanda is for the overworked and overwhelmed—people who move through life fast and struggle to stay connected. Amanda operates primarily through a wearable device affixed to your ear that contains a camera, microphone, GPS, and temperature and heart rate monitor. Amanda then utilizes this data to learn about you and your behavior on social media. Once she is fully trained, she is able to post and interact on social media on your behalf, obtaining content through the wearable device! Amanda operates through three different phases, each with varying levels of user involvement: Learning, Partial Automation, and Total Control. Amanda is a social commentary on our over-dependence on social media. She is a purposefully-flawed solution to a problem that many of us social media users have: spending too much time sharing and curating our lives online at the expense of our privacy and our time (away from technology).

Aidee Cantu
B.A. Cognitive Science, 2017

Jiachen Hu
B.A. Computer Science, 2017

Mane Chakarian
B.A. Psychology and
Interdisciplinary Studies, 2017

Taylor Wong
B.S. Electrical Engineering and
Computer Science, 2018

Faculty Mentor: James Pierce, Jacobs Institute for Design Innovation

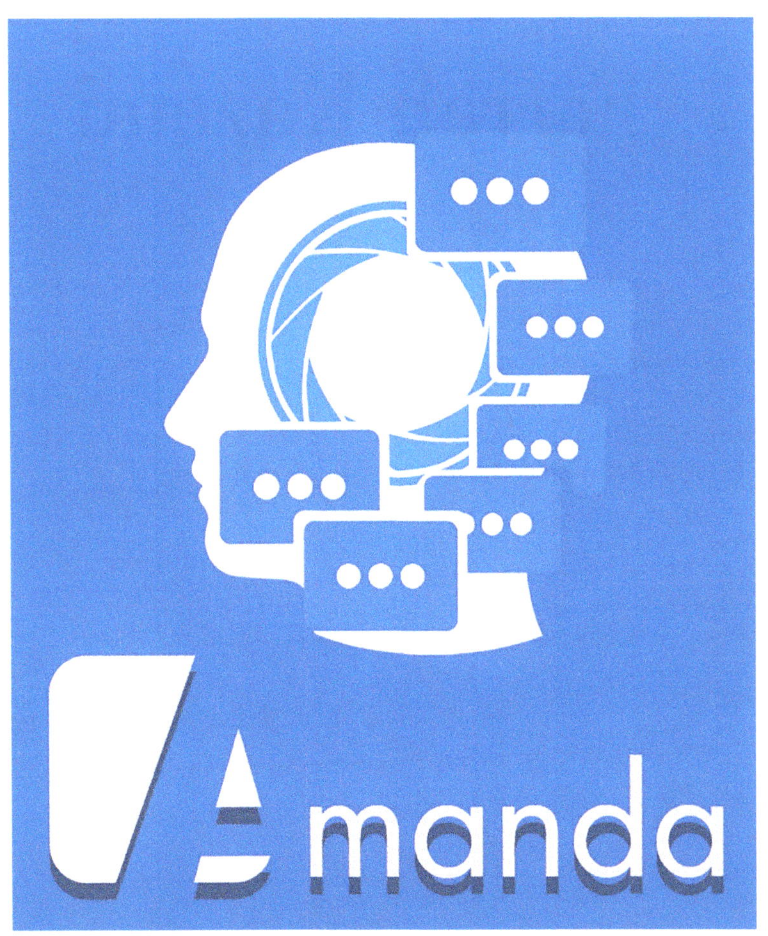

Aidee Cantu, Mane Chakarian, Jiachen Hu, Taylor Wong, *Amanda*, 2017.
Paper poster with designs created in Adobe Creative Suite, 5 posters, each 30 x 45 inches.

Farrah Kazemi

Celeste, a young graphic designer moves to a strange town run by a dictatorial mayor who isn't exactly human. She quickly learns that the town is polarized into two groups—rebellious townspeople in fox masks who roam the town, finding ways to resist through art/expression and the mayor's supporters who do their best to squash resistance in all forms. Celeste gets caught in the crossfire and has to find herself and her place within this strange, rabbit hole world she's fallen into.

Farrah Kazemi
B.A. Film Studies, 2017

Faculty Mentor: J. Mira Koppell, Film & Media Studies

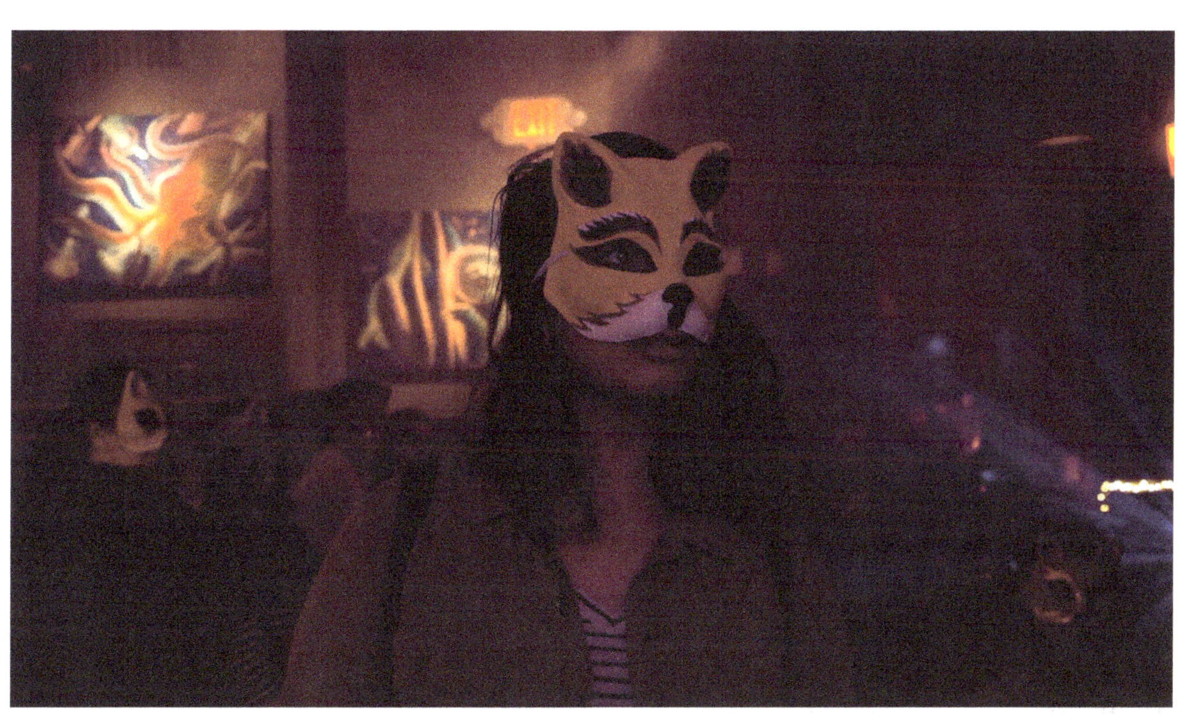

Farrah Kazemi, *Guy Fawkes Day*, 2017. Short film, 14:03 minutes.

DESIGN

Adam Mansour

This piece is drawn in part from a senior thesis entitled, Virtually Chinese: WeChat as a Transnational Digital Space, *which explores how the Chinese social media app WeChat fosters intimate forms of communication through expressively saturated mediums including voice, iconography, and financial transactions. Ultimately, the work compares the mobile app to the concepts of the panopticon, total institutions, and heterotopias. The implications of these conclusions are noted here through the lens of global citizenship; that the internet is channel for global citizenship is a misleading assumption, and designers should be prepared to challenge its effects in their work.*

Adam Mansour
B.A. Anthropology, 2017
Berkeley Design Innovation Certificate, 2017

Faculty Mentor: Terrence Deacon, Anthropology

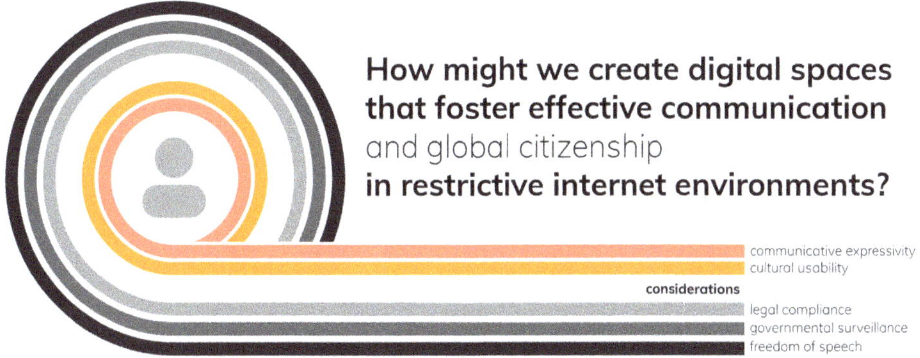

Over the past three decades, internet-based communication platforms have grown at unprecedented rates. Designers have played an essential role in the development and spread of these products. As they shape the world through new technologies, designers have a responsibility to understand the effects of their work globally.

As Keith Murphy, a design anthropologist writes, "one of the primary functions of the design world, in addition to generating economic value for designers through the financial valuation of their work, is to oversee the procedures through which certain classes of objects are made culturally meaningful, and to monitor the social terrain within which those meanings are delimited, elaborated, and contained.... most designers do not see their work as overtly political, though most do subscribe to a general sort of politics of 'care' in their own lives that they would prefer their work to reflect," suggesting an opportunity for us to reconsider the role designers play in technology development.

The speed at which digital products can scale makes the study of their "social terrain" particularly daunting. Not only are profitability and cultural resonance responsibilities of designers, but designers must be attuned to the global settings for which they are designing.

Perhaps the most notable artifact of globalized technology and its effect on social and communicative practices is the spread of the mobile phone, and with it, social media.

While Facebook and WhatsApp have become household names in diverse linguistic and cultural communities, WeChat, the predominant social media platform used in China has not captured a notable market share outside of China (where Facebook and Google are banned). What makes WeChat notable? The app, which is used by nearly a billion individuals, is subject to the Chinese government's surveillance and censorship practices (often referred to as the Great Firewall), even when users are situated outside of China. Outfitted with cultural iconography, including digitized "red packets", which are traditionally gifted on Chinese New Year, WeChat's design fosters forms of culturally-rooted intimacy within a surveilled virtual space.

From the Occupy movement, to the Egyptian Revolution, Brexit, and the elections of Presidents Obama and Trump, social media has undoubtedly played a pivotal role in politics over the past decade. If we are to imagine internet-based communication and social media as channels for global citizenship, we must recognize the designer's role in mitigating risk for users across political, linguistic, and social settings. In what ways are citizens equipped by digital media to voice dissent, express ourselves, and access information? As it is now, WeChat makes its users vulnerable for partaking in such forms of citizenship by consolidating a wide range of functionality in a censored space. Without the ability to communicate openly and safely, these internet users can never be truly global citizens.

By framing designs as contorted reflections of their surrounding social realities (heterotopias, in Foucauldian terms), designers can aim to reflect imagined realities in which global citizenship is accessible to internet users regardless of their geography. Of course this is easier said than done, but by recognizing that the internet is not the same around the world, and by treating it as such, designers might be able to lead the way to creating a safer, more inclusive internet.

Adam Mansour, *Designing Social Media for Global Citizenship*, 2017.

LIVING OBJECTS

Jerome Rivera Pansa

Axis Points *is a performance and installation piece staging conversations of materials as animate beings in a "hosted" space. As a part of the performance, Rivera Pansa drafted and presented a conglomerated lecture with text appropriated from idiosyncratic poetry, queer abstraction catalogs, gender and sexuality academic journals, and Youtube video transcript. The installation space includes objects collected from the street, borrowed mementos, yard sale items, thrifted goods, and discrete sculptures.* Axis Points *presents the authorship of objects with embedded histories and as speakers of their own mythology. Rivera Pansa objectifies within the installation bridging the gray areas between audience participation, material agency, and artist manipulation.* Axis Points *addresses the impermanence of identity, canons, and the fixed through peripheral voices.*

Jerome Rivera Pansa
B.A. Art Practice, 2017
Wendy Sussman Memorial Award in Painting, 2016
and Honors Program Awardee, Fall 2016

Faculty Mentor: Brody Reiman and Anne Walsh, Art Practice

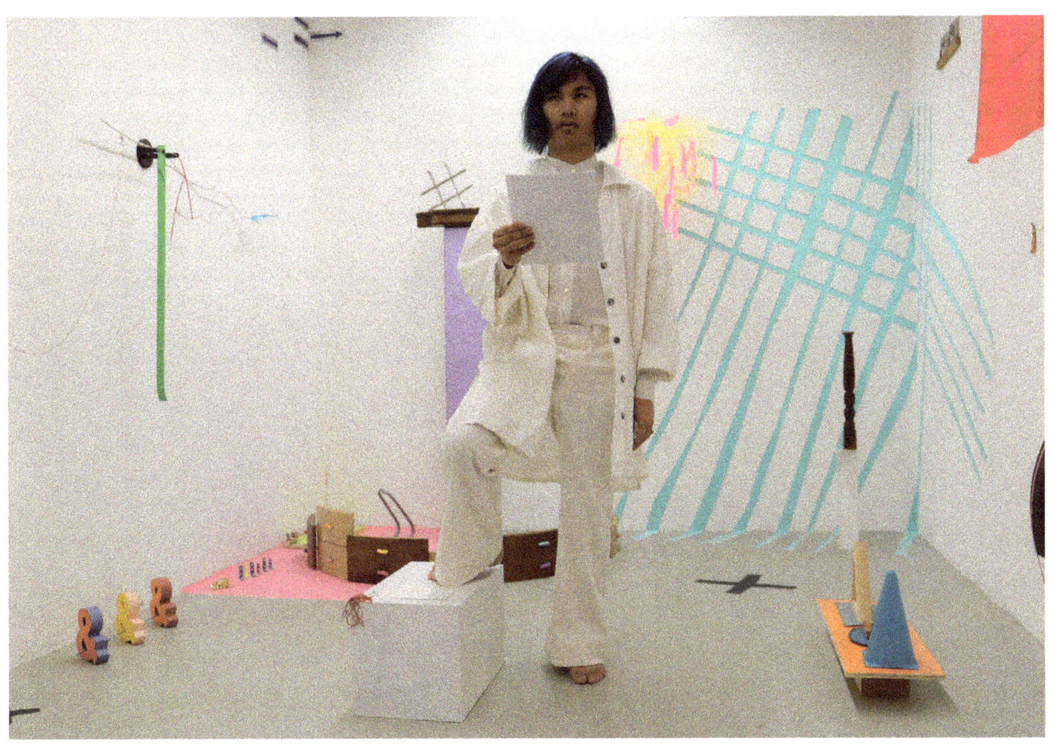

Jerome Rivera Pansa, *Axis Points*, 2016. Performance and installation, duration and dimensions variable. Photo Courtesy: Isabella Manfredi.

Farm-to-Label

We propose that by developing intimate relationships between owner and clothing, we can create a compelling alternative to fast fashion. By cultivating clothing, we found that people become attached to their clothing, and by growing styles, we can accommodate changes in trends with biodegradable, eco-friendly patches. So, we designed a full kit, Farm-to-Label, *that will help anybody grow their own clothing accessories.*

The requirements of the process, including a one week growing time, encourage mindfulness. The smell and the sight of the sprouts invoke excitement, and some studies suggest smells of specific plants can encourage changes in heart rate, breathing, memory and stress levels (aromatherapy).

Ziqi Chen
B.A. Computer Science, 2019

Shail Shah
M.Eng, 2017

Chengcheng Huang
M.Arch, 2018

Michael Singer
M.Eng, 2017

Carlo Liquido
M.S. Information and
Management Systems, 2017

Faculty Mentor: Eric Paulos, Electrical Engineering and Computer Science

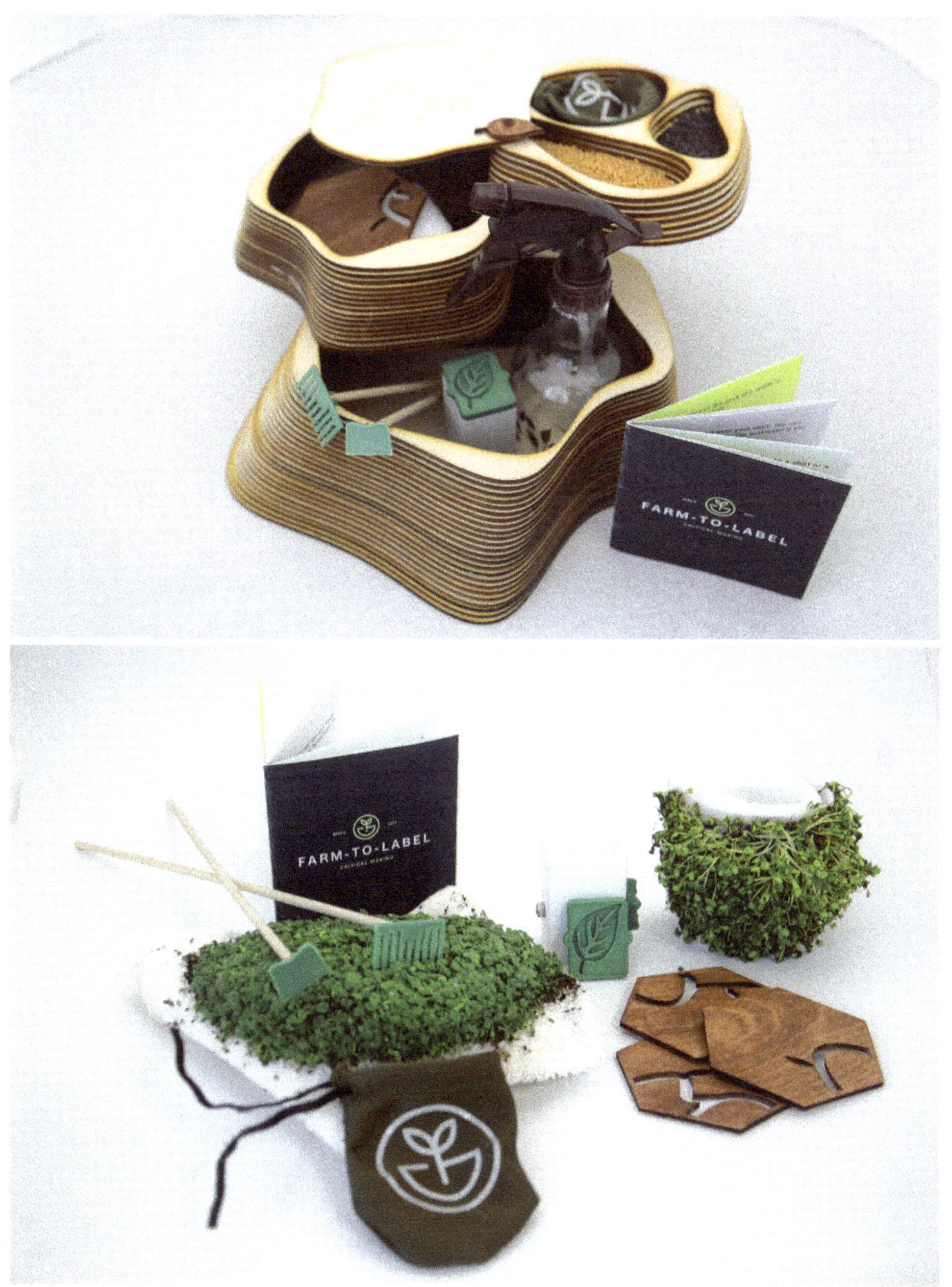

Ziqi Chen, Chengcheng Huang, Carlo Liquido, Shail Shah, Michael Singer, *Farm-to-Label*, 2017.
Live plants (black mustard, yellow mustard, chia), fabric, laser cut wood, 3D printed plastic, 9 x 9 x 6 inches.

Jason Bircea

"How," Susan Stewart asks, in her classic book on the limits of textual representation, "does the present appropriate the past?"

Jason Bircea
B.A. English, 2017
English Departmental Citation, 2017 and McNair Scholar, 2016

Faculty Mentor: Celeste Langan, English

A Nostalgia for the "Mouth"; how Media Technologies (re)stage the absence and return of the Beloved's Voice

A (lover's) PREFACE

Roland Barthes REDUX: *I am the one who waits.*

I caterpillar dream.

I rest beneath a cool, open window, a bottle of dark soda nestled between my knees. Beside me lilacs dance heavy, drunk on homespun moonshine.

Later, I am fat and laid all out over aspen leaves, waiting, smoking *L&M's* in chill sunlight. Waiting for what? My beloved, she has thick, brown hair that cascades down her hips. She is from an island far-off. Her father casts down fish nets there in search of translucent jellyfish.

My daughter is with me now. Her skin is darker than mine, dark like her mother's. She has pebble, brown eyes that crackle noisily, like trampled on leaves. She rests her little head over my shoulders. I rise, pressing the *L&M's* into my back pocket, and walk over to a rose hedge fat with yellow. I pick at it with one hand, hold my daughter up against my chest with the other.

Abruptly I grow old, unfathomably old. I cannot hear or see, but move without moving, move the earth's unmoving way. Yet I must be near the sea. I can taste the ocean's evaporated salt, sweltering in the heat. I press the bottle of dark soda to my lips. It tastes metallic, sandy. There is no sweetness to it.

"How," Susan Stewart asks, in her classic book on the limits of textual representation, "does the present appropriate the past?"

> How does our gaze upon the past, even when articulated as a desire to escape mediation, always separate us from the past? How do aspects of culture become periodized in time just as under tourism they become localized in space? How do certain forms become emblematic of ways of life? (Stewart, 74).

Following Stewart, I am interested in how the "desire to escape mediation"—the desire to, as it were, construct a narrative without recourse to point-of-view (as if one could look back from the position of no-place)—(re-)produces appropriative cultural practices. Stewart has, I think, two senses of "appropriate" in mind. First, and perhaps primarily, the verb/action "to appropriate," to annex or attach an object (to oneself) "as a possession or piece of property;" but also, and somewhat paradoxically, as that which is appropriate in the adjectival sense: that which is "suitable, proper," what (ultimately) "belongs to oneself" (OED). Appropriation, "the making of a thing private property," thus harbors a curious aporia, in which what has been annexed ("rendered subject") is both other and not, outside and in. To ask how the present appropriates the past is thus to foreground the irreducible "gap" between them (Stewart, 74). Indeed, to "gaze upon the past" is to produce that very gap/difference. To appropriate then, is not necessarily to take possession of a thing, but rather to fabricate a (failed) belonging with it. Echoing Walter Benjamin, we might say that the *writing* of history is, as a cultural practice, intrinsically appropriative. Moreover, it is precisely the problem of mediation that I wish in this paper to foreground, particularly in relation to media technology's—including print, phonography, photography, and digital—startling capacity to stage and re-stage the absence and return of the beloved's voice.

The Romantic trope in which the sentimental poet mourns the loss of orality/ the oral world, is an instance of such appropriation/failed belonging. Editor-collector Walter Scott (1771–1832), for instance, theorized the ballad as a repository for what has been lost (in time):"It [popular song] is a chapter in the history of the childhood of society" (Scott, 38). In casting the ballad as an early "chapter" in society's (presumed) linear progression from infancy to full-maturation, Scott re-contextualizes the present through his appropriation of the past; the ballad is "artifactualized," cut from the contingencies of its performative context and refashioned as a signifier for an oral tradition that has been, with the advent of print, presumably lost. Thus, a paradox: the print medium provides the very mechanisms by which one can mourn the loss of orality. Understood as a tissue of citations (with each transcribed ballad *marking* the occasion of an initial oral performance/transmission), the antiquarian's ballad book is a (re)product(ion) of print technology's paradoxical reification of speech), a consequence, that is, of print's appropriation(s) of the (open) mouth. Moreover, in dis-locating the (open) mouth, print technology's representation(s) of voice(s) necessarily foreground the acousmatic dimension of sound. That is, print calls attention to the "mouth's" status as *already* a figure of speech; an orifice, the "O" from which my voice sounds forth, the open mouth is abysmal, a figure of influence/ effluence. Print technologies thus expose, even as they work to foreclose (by way of their displacement of the "mouth") the primordial question: *whence this voice?*

But how exactly does print technology displace the "mouth" (and how ought we to characterize this displacement? As an uncovering, a laying bare, of that which lurks behind the figure of the "mouth"?) Stewart writes of oral form(s) remediation into writing: "...the *writing* of oral genres always results in a residue of lost context and lost presence that literary culture...imbues with a sense of nostalgia and even regret" (Stewart, 104). Crucially then, it is the writing/transcription of oral literature that structures the gap between present and past, print and oral forms—and moreover, foregrounds that irreducible difference as a loss. The cultural work of ballad collection performed by the editor-collector is thus cast as a curious work of mourning that grieves a loss that it itself both produces and announces. But unlike, say, melancholia, in which the lost object often goes un- or mis- recognized, the antiquarian's desire to recover a lost oral world/word is driven by nostalgia, a longing for "home."

Jason Bircea, *A Nostalgia for the "Mouth"; how Media Technologies (re)stage the absence and return of the Beloved's Voice*. Excerpt from research paper, 40 pages, 2017.

Smart Home Devices for the Blind

Our mission statement is "To create an affordable, reliable, and intuitive product to help the visually impaired/blind live more independently at home. Our product will also be useful and desirable to the normally sighted to help it scale economically." After going through a user-centered design process, including user interviews and design iteration we developed a fully functional prototype. The world's first Amazon Alexa controlled smart microwave.

Arshad Ali
B.A. Computer Science, 2017

Stephen Chu
B.S. Mechanical Engineering, 2017

Alex Chong
B.S. Mechanical Engineering and Electrical Engineering and Computer Science, 2017

Yudi Sun
B.A. Sociology, 2018

Faculty Mentor: Euiyoung Kim, Jacobs Institute for Design Innovation

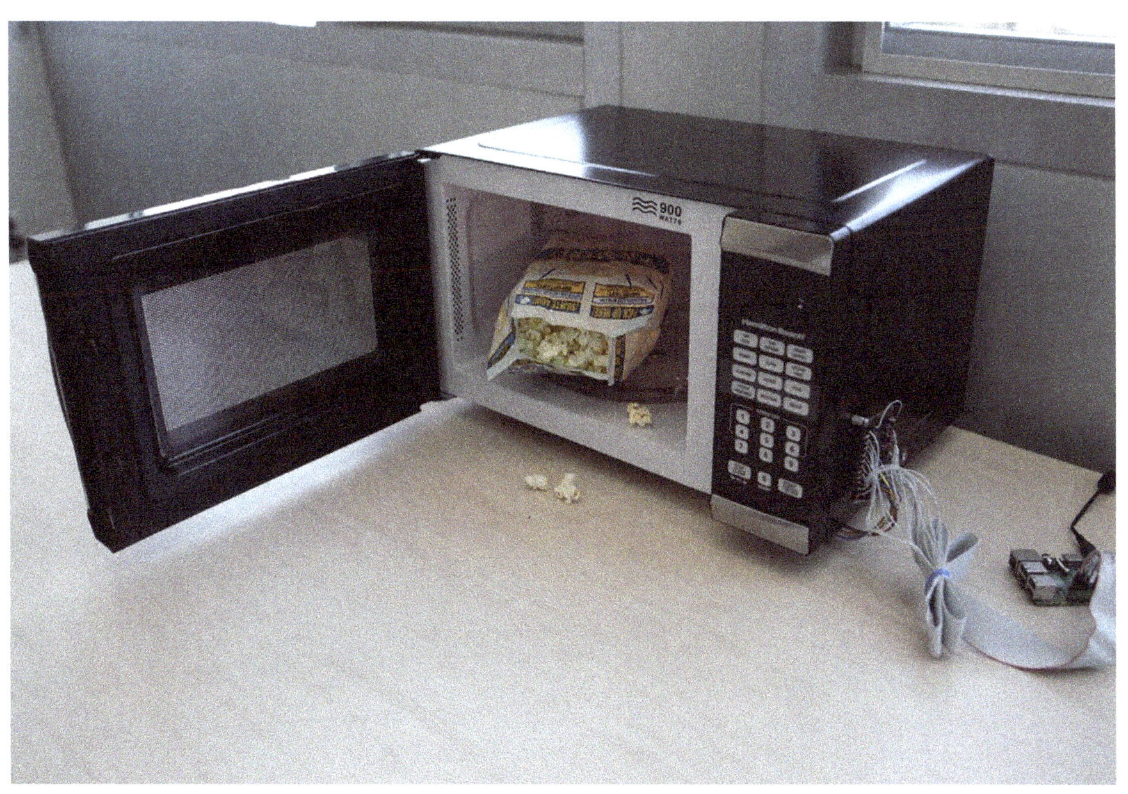

Arshad Ali, Alex Chong, Stephen Chu, Yudi Sun, *Smart Home Devices for the Blind*, 2017.User centered design, Amazon Echo, Raspberry Pi, electronics, 2 x 2 x 2 feet.

Principal Power Buoy

After two physical prototypes and 3.6 Million mathematical models, we designed a 1:3.333 scale exact model of a wifi generating, surf-data-collecting Principal Power Buoy. It is self-sustaining, eco-friendly, user-friendly, and effective. It can float in water, remain stable through waves, send wifi signals, and tell users about the ocean.

On the software side, the animation showcases the users journey through the website that provides the data to surfers, exhibits our sponsor, and logs our users into the wifi.

Hunter Garnier
B.S. Mechanical Engineering, 2018

Stephanie Mah
B.S. Mechanical Engineering, 2017

Akhilesh Mishra
B.S. Mechanical Engineering, 2018

Beshoy Wabha
B.S. Mechanical Engineering, 2018

Alexander Wing
B.A. Economics, 2018

Albert Zhou
B.S. Mechanical Engineering, 2018

Faculty Mentor: Euiyoung Kim, Jacobs Institute for Design Innovation

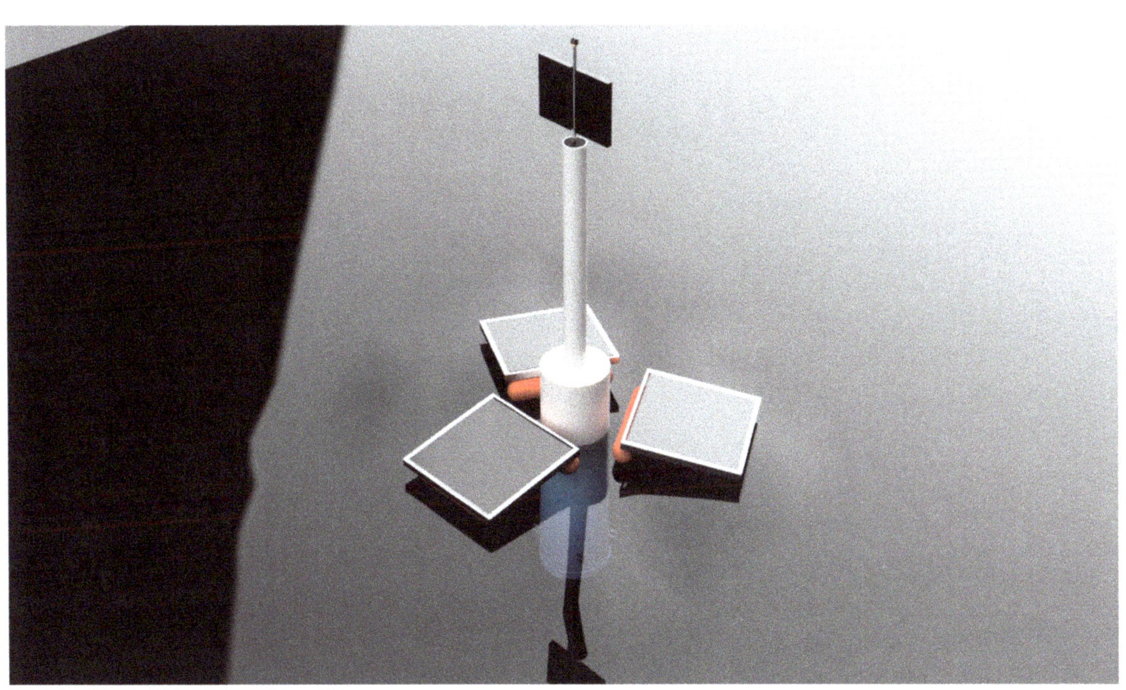

Hunter Garnier, Stephanie Mah, Akhilesh Mishra, Beshoy Wabha, Alexander Wing, Albert Zhou, *Principal Power Buoy.* Animation, poster, PVC, electric buoy, 3 ½ x 1 foot.

Fetal and Maternal Health Monitoring

Our goal was to develop a fetal health monitoring system that was accurate, safe, and highly usable in the comfort of a home. This vision took the form of a stretchable, wearable device that monitored baby vitals in real time, relaying the data to doctors and providing mothers with peace of mind by avoiding specialized care visits during pregnancy.

Tushar Mittal
B.S. Chemical Biology and Material Science, 2018

Arbaaz Shakir
B.S. Mechanical Engineering, 2018

Faculty Mentors: Euiyoung Kim, Jacobs Institute for Design Innovation

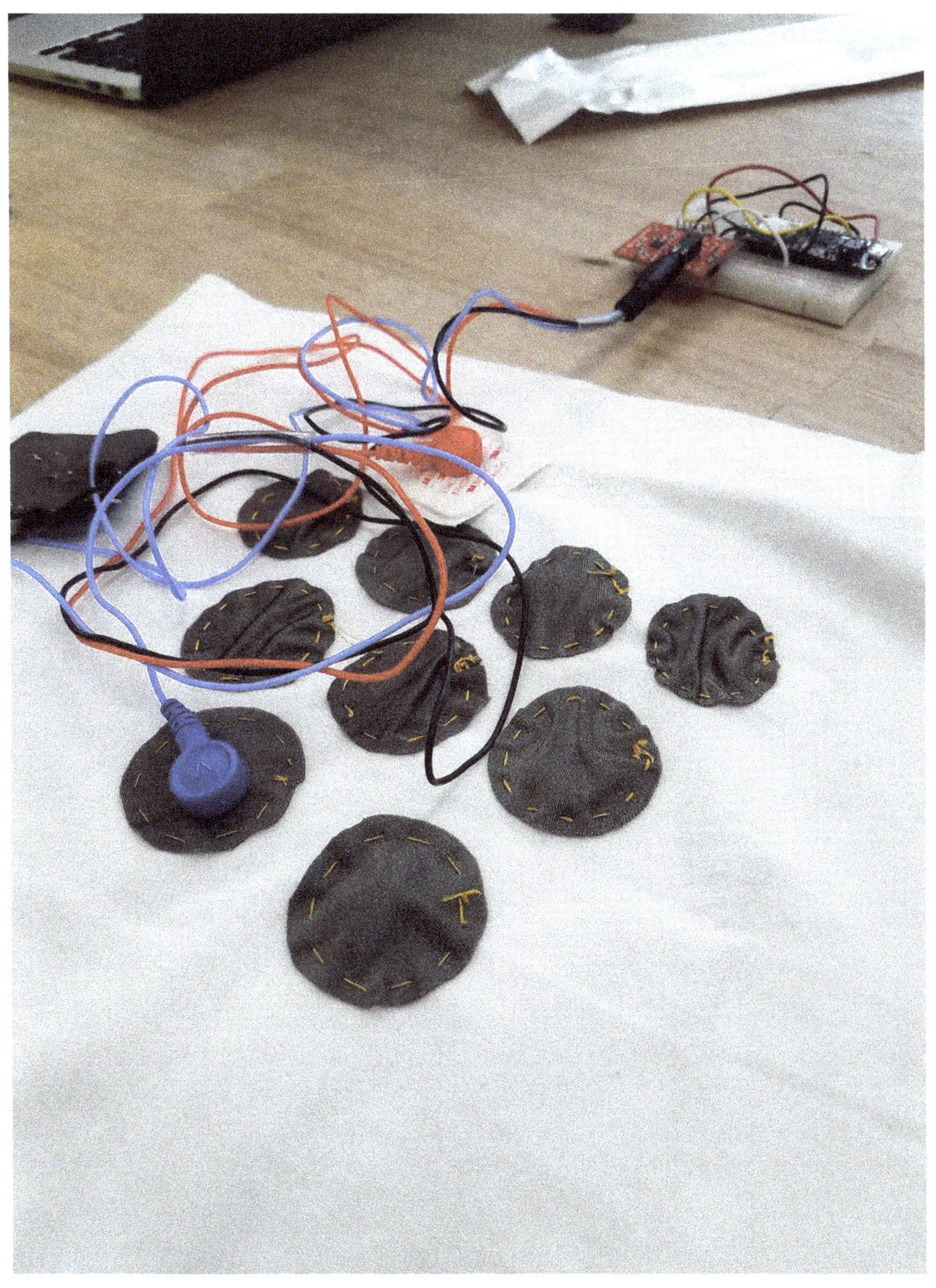

Tushar Mittal, Arbaaz Shakir, *Fetal and Maternal Health Monitoring*, 2017.
Working prototype on fabric, 18 inches (width).

Belinda Cortez

For this piece I have casted a sculpture out of aluminum. Some of the aluminum material being used for the cast is from beer cans that were consumed by myself, family, and friends while engaging in conversations. This is an important element of my project as I feel that the interactions and conversations are carried conceptually through the material used in the piece. I recorded some of the conversations and, after listening to them, was inspired to sculpt what I would be casting. In this case, it was an anatomical heart. One of the conversations I listened to a few times was my mom's story in which she was re-telling us about her upbringing within poverty in rural Mexico and her long journey to the United States. Thinking about the sacrifices she and women specifically in my family continue to take inspired the imagery for the mural component of my piece. The nopales (cacti) depicted relate to survival in a harsh environment and have also been the food and medicine of many indigenous peoples including my family. The mobility of this double-sided wall, which is able to roll on wheels, represents the migration and sacrifices that people have taken on to create opportunities for survival. These investigations and the ongoing longing to connect and know more about my ancestral cultural practices inspired the overall piece.

Belinda Cortez
B.A. Art Practice, 2017
Eisner Prize, 2017

Faculty Mentor: Brody Reiman, Art Practice

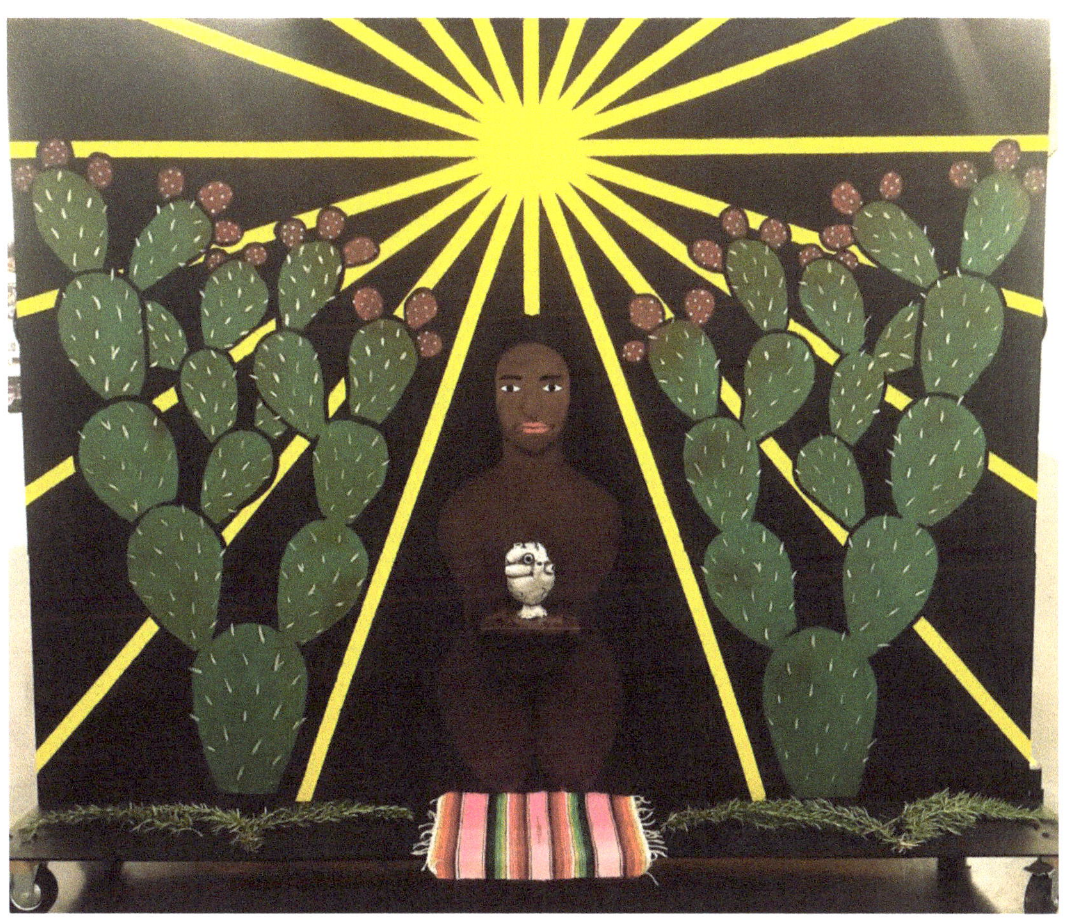

Belinda Cortez, *Energias Cosmicas*, 2017. Mixed media, acrylic on panel, casted aluminum, audio, dimensions variable.

Aileen Candelario

Nature neither sees nor creates borders—only man does; and just as butterflies journey from area to area—so does man. A Monarch's Migration acts as a visual metaphor for human migration and attempts to further explore the workings of this universal movement. It examines the reasoning behind this natural development while ultimately aiming to showcase the many struggles encountered during such transition.

Aileen Candelario
B.A. Art Practice and Journalism, 2018
Eisner Prize, 2017 and Honors Studio, 2017

Faculty Mentor: Azin Seraj, Art Practice

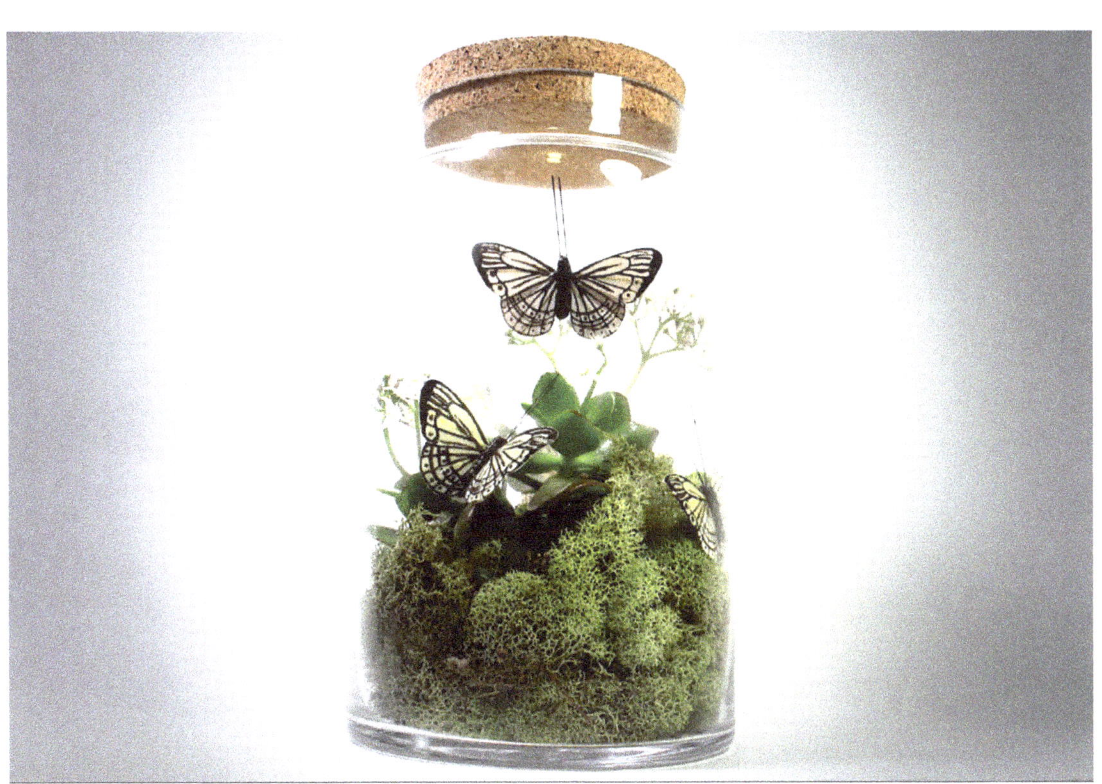

Aileen Candelario, *Mi Migracion*, 2016. Stop motion animation video, 5:17 minutes.

Sasha Kudler

This piece (or rather, essay) is an analytical exploration of James Joyce's use of musical allusion and musical language in "The Dead." A talented musician in his own right, Joyce's tendency to reference and approximate music in his works is as brilliant as it is beautiful. With that in mind, this paper seeks to examine how Joyce references and approximates music throughout the short story, paying particular attention to the ways in which these musical moments further the sense of paralysis Joyce cultivates throughout the entirety of Dubliners.

Sasha Kudler
B.A. Music and English, 2017
Chauncey Wetmore Wells Critical Essay Prize, 2017

Faculty Mentor: Jeffrey Blevins, English

Distant Music: Paralysis and Musical Allusion in Joyce's "The Dead"

> He wanted to cry but not for himself: for the words, so beautiful and sad, like music.
>
> —James Joyce, *A Portrait of the Artist as a Young Man*

Although Joyce's *Dubliners* is full of music from start to finish, there's no doubt that "The Dead" is the most overtly musical story in the collection. At nearly sixteen-thousand words, of course, "The Dead" is less a story and more a novella, revisiting and reemphasizing themes and motifs that have run throughout *Dubliners* as a whole. If we regard *Dubliners* itself as a *bildungsroman*, then "The Dead" represents the end of a lifetime of growth, bringing the narrative beyond maturity and into the land of the deceased, a land which all of Ireland, living or otherwise, seems to inhabit. Its musicality, like the musicality of *Dubliners* as a whole, falls into three basic categories: non-diegetic music, diegetic music, and text that approximates and approaches music. While these categories take drastically different forms throughout the text, they do have one thing in common—with each, Joyce explores the tension between music's paralytic and cathartic potentials. Although Joyce utilizes musical allusions and musical language to trap his characters within their own romantic notions of themselves, music also seems, in the case of "The Dead," to be the only force with the power to set them free from this paralysis.

In discussing Joyce's allusive style, it is best to begin by engaging with his non-diegetic musical references, since those are often the easiest to overlook. *Non-diegetic*, in this case, means music which is mentioned in the text, but does not occur within the action of the plot, i.e. music that is not heard or played by the characters. These non-diegetic allusions can range from music that is explicitly mentioned by the characters (for instance, "Yes! Let Me Like a Soldier Fall") to music that is alluded to, often with great subtly, by the narrator or author himself.

One such example of this subtle allusion occurs not within "The Dead," but in the title itself. According to various sources, "Oh, Ye Dead!" a song from Thomas Moore's *Irish Melodies*, provided the inspiration for both the story's title and its contents, setting up a framework through which the entirety of "The Dead" can be viewed. The lyrics of the song, which was originally composed in the early 1800s, are as follows:

> Oh, ye Dead! oh, ye Dead! whom we know by the light you give
> from your cold gleaming eyes, though you move like men who
> live. Why leave you thus your graves,
> In far off fields and waves,

Where the worm and the sea-bird only know your
bed, To haunt this spot where all
Those eyes that wept your fall
And the hearts that wail'd you, like your own, lie dead?

It is true, it is true, we are shadows cold and wan;
And the fair and the brave whom we lov'd on earth are
gone, But still thus ev'n in death,
So sweet the living breath
Of the fields and the flow'rs in our youth we wander'd
o'er That ere, condemn'd, we go
To freeze 'mid Hecla's snow,
We would taste it awhile, and think we live once more![1]

Right from the get-go, the similarities between Moore's song and Joyce's own story are readily apparent. In this song, the dead are not confined to their graves, but wander among the living; the living, therefore, are living amongst the dead. In Joyce's story, the characters are constantly haunted by the ghosts of their past, particularly in the case of Gretta's former beau, Michael Furey, whose spirit returns briefly to the land of the living through song.

Outside of thematic similarities, it's a well-documented fact that Joyce was enamored with Moore's melody—so much so that he asked his brother Stanislaus for a copy of the music, which he "both memorized and sang."[2] The song, like many other popular Irish tunes, is written in D major, and the graceful ornamentation and lilting melody distract somewhat from the tristesse of its lyrics. Interestingly, Joyce's story proceeds with a similar tenor: although the narrative itself is plagued by the dead, the story is superficially a happy (or at least social) one, taking place as it does at a holiday dance. The formal elements of the music, therefore, reflect the formal elements of the evening, providing a civil, conventional tone with a sinister undercurrent. In "The Dead," Joyce's characters are as close to death as the dead are to living—and perhaps even the author's prose, fascinated as it is with Moore's work, is in some ways paralyzed, plagued by the ghost of an artist championed by the Irish Literary Revival. In considering which author he should reference in the speech he will give at dinner, Gabriel reflects that his selection of Robert Browning was a mistake: something more popular, from "Shakespeare or from the Melodies would [have been] better."[3] In comparison to Browning, who influenced such authors as Ezra Pound and T.S. Eliot, Gabriel clearly considers Moore's tome to be plebian, or at least proletarian, a literature fit for general consumption, without Browning's high-brow or academic distinction. In basing his own story off a song from *Irish Melodies*, then, it might seem as though Joyce intended to betray the extent to which his own work, or at least its subjects, can be considered kitsch as opposed to true art. But then again, perhaps it is precisely this re-appropriation that allows Joyce's text to be so effective, giving the reader a glimpse not only of how Dublin is, but how it sees itself, rather than deferring to the projected ideals of foreign artistic influence.

Diegetic music (i.e., music included in the action of the story) has a similar effect on the narrative arc of "The Dead," but is perhaps slightly more poignant than Joyce's non-diegetic examples. Bartell D'Arcy's performance of "The Lass of Aughrim" is without a doubt the most poignant musical moment, not only in "The Dead," but in all of *Dubliners*. Standing engulfed in darkness at the top of the Morkans' staircase, Gretta is the only character who can make out the hoarse music of Mr. D'Arcy who, despite his earlier protestations, is performing the song for the remaining party. Her reaction, simultaneously personal and universal, is unironically provocative in a manner to which Joyce's reader is unaccustomed. As she stands "near the top of the first flight, in shadow... there was grace and mystery in her attitude as though she were a symbol of something."[4] The music, reawakening Gretta's long forgotten memory, is so transformative that she ceases to be a secondary character, and momentarily takes her place at the center of the text.[5] No longer simply imbued with metaphorical potential, for a moment she becomes a metaphor in and of herself. In fact, she becomes so saturated with meaning and symbolic potential that Gabriel, watching with admiration, also appears to experience an awakening, and imagines turning the scene itself into a work of art. Although Mr. D'Arcy is quite sick, and sings with a tenor "made plaintive by distance and by the singer's hoarseness,"[6] his voice touches Gretta to her core: it is as though Michael Furey, far away and long dead, is singing to her from the grave. As Gretta's soul descends into the land of the dead towards the ghost of her late lover, her body comes back to life, with "colour on her cheeks... and her eyes shining."[7] The lyrics, as remembered by Joyce's wife, begin with these verses:

> If you'll be the lass of Aughrim
> As I am taking you mean to be
> Tell me the first token
> That passed between you and me.
>
> O don't you remember
> That night on yon lean hill

When we both met together
Which I am sorry now to tell.

The rain falls on my yellow locks
And the dew it wets my skin;
My babe lies cold within my arms:
Lord Gregory let me in.[8]

In this song, which tells the tale of a young woman robbed of her honor by a cold and distant lord, there are some immediate parallels between this young woman and Michael Furey—after all, both arrived at the houses of their beloved shivering, inconsolable, and soaking wet. Even Gabriel has his place in this narrative; as Ruth Bauerle (who has compiled every song Joyce ever mentioned or sang) notes, "Michael and Gretta are creatures of the rain; but Gabriel, like Lord Gregory, prefers the sheltered life: galoshes for his wife and himself, and a Dublin hotel room rather than a cold trip home by cab in wintry weather."[9] If Gabriel plays Lord Gregory in this rendition of the song, it is no wonder he feels so removed—and even perhaps excluded—from his wife's emotional outburst. Another parallel can easily be drawn between Michael Furey and the young Galway patriot from Yeats' *Cathleen Ni Houlihan*, a play Joyce references with some frequency throughout *Dubliners.* In the play, Cathleen, the embodiment of Ireland, laments a young martyr much like Michael, claiming "he died for love of me: many a man has died of love of me."[10] In this narrative, once again, Gabriel is but a specter, existing at best as a secondary character, perhaps one of the men who have yet to decide whether they will give up their lives for the woman (or country) they love.

Even after this moment of revitalization, of course, Gretta is still among those living who, lulled to sleep by the cold, slumber among the dead. After breaking into tears, she falls asleep, and the falling snow returns her to her paralysis, blanketing graves and rooftops swiftly and equally. One might be tempted, in light of this, to take a rather pessimistic view of the song, regarding it as yet another example of failed provocation, since despite Gretta's apparent revival, she is ultimately frozen in purgatory alongside the rest of her countrymen. For the reader, who has been conditioned by Joyce to expect irony rather than relatability, this interpretation is certainly an arguable one. In spite of this irony, however, it is clear that this song, sung in a stereotypical Irish tenor, somehow achieved what Mary Jane's academy piece, despite its virtuosity, could not. Although Gretta's awakening is short-lived, much like the one Gabriel experiences when he hears Aunt Julia's song, it is undeniable that for a brief instant, these characters were transported beyond the crushing ennui and uncertainty of their day-to-day lives, given, for even the shortest moment, hope that a human project, art in this instance, could truly transport its audience.

Although music seems, at many moments in "The Dead," to be just another paralyzing force, it is also one of the only sources of catharsis, or at the very least release, that the reader finds throughout the entirety of the text. Joyce's musical allusions, both diegetic and non-diegetic, may have the power to paralyze his characters within the confines of pre-existing narratives, but there's no doubt that music, and perhaps art in general, has the capacity to free its audience, at least temporarily, from the land of the dead, a land which everyone in Dublin is otherwise doomed to inhabit.

Works Cited

Bauerle, Ruth. *The James Joyce Songbook*. New York and London: Garland Publishing, 1982.

Gifford, Don. *Joyce Annotated: Notes for Dubliners and A Portrait of the Artist as a Young Man 2nd ed.* Berkeley: University of California Press, 1982.

Haas, Robert. *Music in Dubliners*. Colby Quarterly, Volume 28, no.1, March 1992.

Joyce, James ed. Davies, Laurence. *Dubliners*. Hertfordshire, UK: Wordsworth Editions Ltd., 1993.

Weaver, Jack W. *Joyce's Music and Noise: Theme and Variation in His Writings*. Gainsville, Florida: University Press of Florida, 1998.

Endnotes

1 Ruth Bauerle, ed., *The James Joyce Songbook* (New York and London: Garland Publishing, 1982), 172.

2 *Ibid*, 168.

3 Joyce, 129.

4 Joyce, 151.

5 Robert Haas, *Music in Dubliners* (Colby Quarterly, Volume 28, no.1, March 1992), 31.

6 Joyce, 151.

7 *Ibid*, 151.

8 Gifford, 122.

9 Bauerle, 177.

10 Gifford, 125.

Sasha Kudler, *Distant Music: Paralysis and Musical Allusion in Joyce's* The Dead.
Excerpt from research paper, 16 pages, 2016.

Katie Revilla

Marks/Moments/Time examines my relationship to ideas of labor and production through generations of my family. Using tools that have been passed down to me from my father and grandfather, the rust that now takes over the object is what I use to dye the silk fabric. In both generations of my family, these tools are a symbol for the work they did to support their families, and to offer a better life than the ones they were given when they first emigrated from the Philippines. The work they did in maintaining acres of fields, and the deterioration of these objects is a representation of the invisibility that comes with manual labor. Imprinting the silk by laying the objects onto the rust, these tools become archived and memorialized in the way they are now stained into the fabric. As the metal alloys from the rust begin to eat away at the silk, the prints will slowly shift and change throughout the piece, creating new images and marks. Just as time deteriorates memory, I look at this piece as a living landscape of their lives.

Katie Revilla
B.A. Art Practice, 2017

Faculty Mentor: Allan deSouza, Art Practice

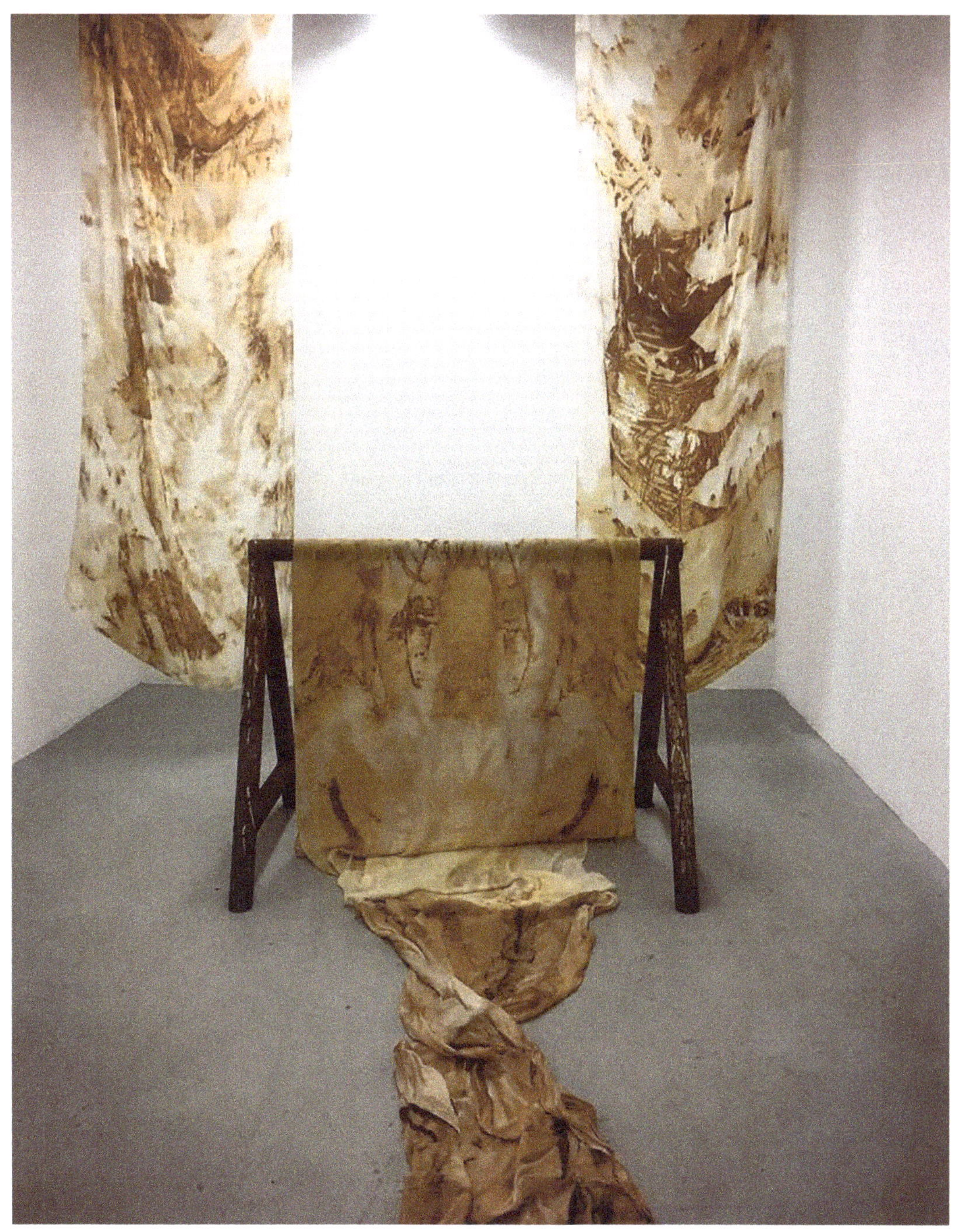

Katie Revilla, *Marks/Moments/Time*, 2017.
Rust from my grandfather's and father's tools on silk, 13 x 12 x 24 feet.

INSIDE AND OUT

GABE CARR
KATHERINE BASU
ZHOUSHU ZIPORYN
LIGHTS IN TENSEGRITY
WHEELSENSE
ARVIN TANU
KRISTEN WILSON
MOLLIE SITZER

Gabe Carr

This past winter, the road that leads to my parents' house collapsed. After a heavy rain, the earth underneath the road filled with water, and it slid right into the creek. There was no returning the displaced dirt. It had turned to mud and slid all the way down the creek to the ocean. It happened fast, over the course of a couple days, so a slab of asphalt on the road's surface, about fifty feet across, dropped straight down. The road that I thought I knew so well had a completely new face, now all raw, exposed rock and earth. In this new face I saw all of the things I hadn't known about the road. I had a dream in which I squatted to the ground, then touched my cheek to the golden divider lines. From this angle, it looked like there was no gap—the two pairs of lines seemed to connect across the crater.

This event showed me that the road was like an image. I had only ever come in contact with its surface. Eye/image, eye/person, tires/ asphalt, knife/skin, they are all like meeting someone for the first time—everything is contact, a meeting at the surface. Stories of first contact are told and retold, and past encounters find themselves in imagined futures. But surface doesn't always mean shallowness. Surface also acts as a verb meaning to bring to/to come to the surface, suggesting depth through which the body or an object can move, and also a revelation of latent histories. In a future dream, two golden strangers will come from outer space to meet each other here, across the crater.

Gabe Carr
B.A. Art Practice, 2017

Faculty Mentors: Allan deSouza and Randy Hussong, Art Practice

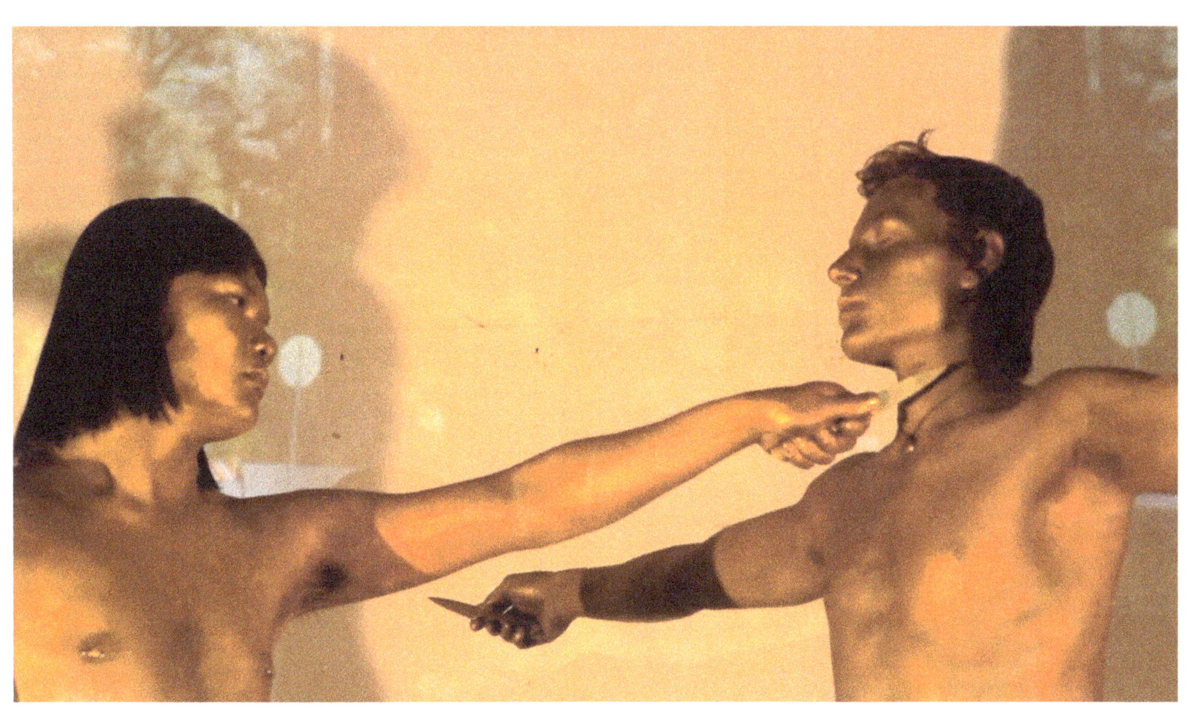

Gabe Carr, *CONTACT, CLEARING*, 2017. Video, screenprint, 5:51 minutes, 18 x 38 inches.

Katherine Basu

My design responded to "Surviving the MULTI", choreographed by Andrea Olivares and danced by Melissa Chapman. This piece related to the multiplicity of roles that a woman is expected to take on over the course of her life, showing metaphorically the journey of a woman from childlike wonder to mature passion and balance.

It was clear to me that the piece crescendoed as Melissa's portrayal of "woman" matured, and I chose to let my design parallel that build. I began the piece with Melissa playing with small lights under a table, revealing her in dim, neutral light. More saturated looks, featuring bold colors, silhouettes, and sidelight were introduced in the more chaotic sections of the piece to mirror the passionate tone of the movement. Because of the many shifts in tone and rhythm, the design oscillated between sharp changes and fluid transitions, following Melissa's movements.

My intent was ultimately for the design to create, not only a visual field to contextualize the piece for the audience, but also to offer an immersive, dynamic environment for the dancer to inhabit as well, rendering the work more cohesive and compelling.

Katherine Basu
B.A. Theater, Dance and Performance Studies, 2017
Roselyn Schneider Eisner Prize for Continuing Creative Achievement, 2017

Faculty Mentor: Jack Carpenter, Theater, Dance and Performance Studies

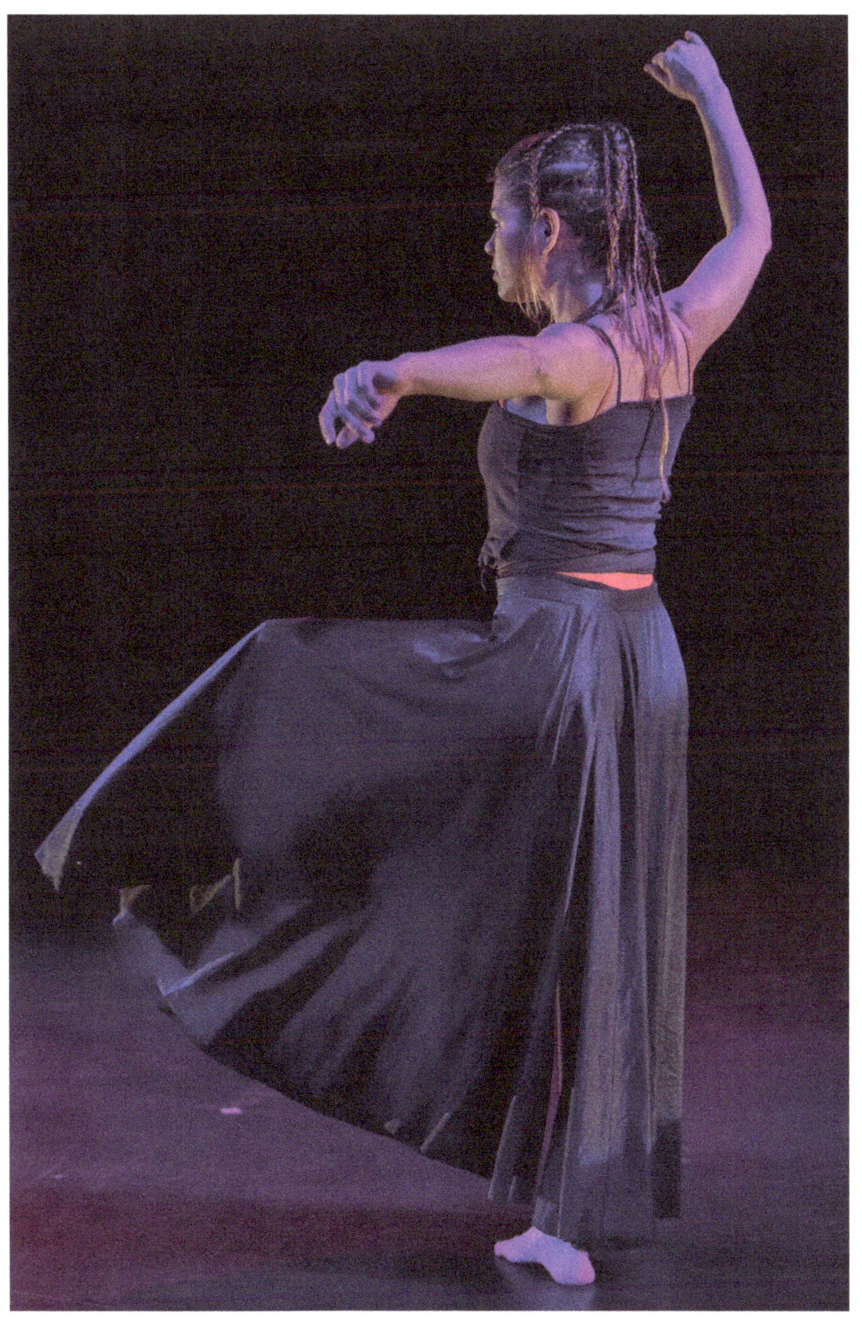

Katherine Basu, *Lighting and Stage Design for Choreography Showcase 2016*. Live performance, 8 minutes

Zhoushu Ziporyn

Star Wars Palimpsest *is an original musical theatre/film, post-modern cantata work that pits the parallels between the cosmology of the Star Wars movies with the story of Abraham and Isaac in the Bible, as a kind of postmodern cantata that aims to provoke further flexibility of thought. The work is a philosophical commentary farce that retells the saga of the Star Wars films, a social phenomenon of deep and undiminished fandom that seems to have resonated abidingly with the cultural unconscious and can galvanize communities, as a commentary on the politics of freedom of thought, specifically, of religious indoctrination and oppression. It is not about whose side to take, but ultimately about the individual's critical freedom of thought devoid of emotional distortion and indoctrination, free of moral dualism and its concomitant extremism.*

Zhoushu Ziporyn
B.A. Music and Philosophy, 2017
Honors Thesis

Faculty Mentor: Ken Ueno, Music

Forward

With Trump's triumph in the 2016 election, the United States faces the future as an ever more divided and polarized nation. As Trump's demagoguery and bigotry continues to stir up the nation and the globe, the fear of fascism and dangerous social and political consequences of fanaticism and dogmatic faith have become evermore pertinent. The common driving force in our polarized political climate, especially in Trump's campaign, can perhaps be described as a pervasive ethos of "us against them," expressed as blind faith and fanaticism. It is now a pressing challenge to locate the crux of this problem at its very roots, to seek out what is most philosophically fundamental in grounding these dangerous trends in America's contemporary thought.

While on the surface it seems like the problem here is the farce that is the insatiable rise of the extremist Right with Trump's campaign, the real essence of the problem lies neither in the Republicans nor in the Democrats per se, but in the very idea of extremism in both. This basic "us against them" mentality that assumes that the opponent is ipso facto wrong. Liberalism and progressivism have their strength in their openness and tolerance toward difference and disagreement. The irony here is that progressivism seems to fail its own test when it becomes too extreme and becomes convinced that its way of thinking and doctrine is ~~in the~~ right and that those who disagree with it are wrong. We need a platform for conversation, not adamant displays of disapproval and hostile black-and-white labeling against the opposing side.

Given that this extremism seems to be the ultimate driving force dividing our nation, we now need to think outside the box and find its source at its very root. My claim is that extremism is rooted in the fundamental metaphysical assumption of the existence of an absolute good, a substantialist conception of goodness that undergirds a "more is better" moral-dualism. It is the idea that if something is good, then necessarily having more or doing more of this goodness, extirpating as much as possible of whatever is not it (whatever is deemed to be different from it), will inevitably be even more good. And this only works if you assume that there is somehow an absolute goodness ~~inhering~~ inherent in things ~~in~~ themselves, independent of their context and application. The extremist believes that if they keep doing more and more of what ~~they~~ he/she think is right, it will necessarily be for the better and bring a net increase in good. But as we have seen in our current political culture, this has been shown to be false. Upon sober reflection, I believe we can see that, in crucial respects, the goodness of things is largely if not entirely dependent upon their relation to their total environment, and maximized by relations of balance and moderation. The contrary faith in the absolute good, of moral-dualism, is so ingrained that it by now seems almost the default assumption of universal and unavoidable common sense. But that is not the case; this conception has a specific cultural history: tracing it to its ultimate origins, it is, to put it bluntly, an inheritance of specific Platonic and monotheistic doctrines. In all these texts, the assumption is that if X is good, more X is better—and further, the failure to be radically extreme in the commitment to one's conception of goodness is a damnable vice.

Religious fanaticism in its latent structural form, rather than its explicit doctrinal form, seems to be the key to Trump's success, where rationality and reason is trumped by faith and unchecked conviction.

As Carolyn Chen's case study of Taiwanese immigrants and their religious experience attests, immigrants into the US find themselves extremely vulnerable and in need of a community (Chen 38). The tragedy here is that they can't help but seek refuge in certain religious doctrines which provide an on-the-surface welcoming community, and before they know it, they are also submitting to a very specific indoctrination of belief, propagating the aforementioned problem we face today even more (Chen 186). In the face of this neo-colonial expansion of the structures of moral-dualism to unsuspecting hosts, my piece wants to reassert the increasingly endangered understanding that moral-dualism is one among many ways of looking at the universe, and that it is in no way absolute. That does not mean we want to eliminate it, however. On the contrary, we in fact need a whole spectrum of viewpoints, not a black-and-white opposition. My mission with this piece is therefore to create, or at least spark, alternative communities that are devoid of commitments to religious indoctrination, to resist the normalization of moral-dualism as the default structure of all cultural thinking. Through the mechanism of popular culture, we need to build a bridge between the polarities, and make a place of safety and trust, through the arts as education, to facilitate people to think and talk with each other.

ABRAHAM (Cont.)

You don't understand the power of the Ecclesia. In order to achieve great things, some sacrifice must be made. I must obey my master. That will be the true testimony of my faith.

ISAAC

Well, let it be known that I will not be converted. And you will be forced to kill me in the name of Japer.

ABRAHAM

If that is what Japer intends...

ISAAC

Search, father. I feel the sense arousing clouds within you! Let go of your blind faith!

ABRAHAM

(pause, then pensively) It is too late for me, son. *(authoritatively and resolutely)* To have order, we must sort things. To put each thing in its rightful category. Otherwise, there is chaos. And that is why we need an institution to oversee this. And it is no easy task, that. We must acquire any resource possible to aid this grand goal. Japer will show you the truth about the universe. He is your master now.

ISAAC

(with deep grief but also in a somewhat threatening tone)
Then my father is truly gone.
(daringly) It is then him against me now.

ABRAHAM

I find your lack of faith disturbing.

ABRAHAM and ISAAC face slightly away from each other, but an angle so that they can still see each other in their peripheral vision.

One spotlight on each. ISAAC does not respond to ABRAHAM's words, but ABRAHAM sings the last 6 bars of "Isaac, He Laughs" as a monologue.

"He laughs, he laughs! And I cry with him. I understand. He laughs, And I cry, I cry, I cry." Spotlight now only on ABRAHAM. It is in his mind; ISAAC cannot hear it. Once ABRHAM finishes singing, spotlight shines only on ISAAC, and he sings "Dear Japer" [Track 13]. ABRAHAM cannot hear this either. As the tune fades out, so do the lights.)

Lyrics to "Dear Japer" [Track 13]:

Dear great Japer
Won't you hear my prayer
Tell me please, how you play your dare Even with you there. Are you there?
Call me soon! Where's my father?
My forsaken mast in the monsoon Waves in wrath create the calm ocean Reflects back what it wants
My ship stares back to the moonlight Killing the fly on the starboard
O Japer
Even as the rivers flow You may be my foe
You may take my land Or simply take my hand But you will never Take my father forever

As I sail the sea
I see things that I would never see Had I stayed in my land far away.
And I used to be principled like you for a day Now across the sea!
The winds are loud and make me cold. Shores of green and gold.
Its forsaken mast needs not words Wind alone propels
But your words nudged them to harness the wind The ship is light compared to the sea
But not me, no not me, no not me. Even as the blood flows

You may be what glows You may take the steeple Even tame my people
But you will never Print your lies onto me Even as the stakes rise You may take the prize You may take my pride Even take a friend
But you will never
Carve my reality. Not for me

if it started as a prank You may take the rank You may take the power Even take a shower
But you will never
Imprint your theme onto me

Even if I will be slayed I won't run away
I will be loyal
To my father's toil But you will never
Take me any where. Not from here

Forming it in instant jest You may have the best Grabble in all the boons Send
down the typhoons
But you will never
Take my sense from me. From me

Even though you brought it up You may drink the cup
Even take their hearts
But who knows where it starts But you will never
Take my thoughts from me. from me Even take the arts

(BLACK OUT) (END OF SCENE)(END OF ACT)

Zhoushu Ziporyn, *Star Wars Palimpsest*, 2017.
Live performance, 50:43 minutes.

Lights in Tensegrity (LiT)

We designed LiT *through the class ME 110: Introduction to Product Development. In collaboration with Berkeley Emergent Space Tensegrities (BEST) Lab, NASA Ames has been developing tensegrity soft robots for space exploration. Our industry sponsor, BEST lab, prompted us to discover alternative uses for these tensegrity structures. We used a Human Centered Design approach to brainstorm novel ideas, including responsive architecture, modular, ergonomic architecture and STEM educational kits. Finally, we devised the concept of dynamic, responsive and kinetic lighting structures. We developed* Lights in Tensegrity (LiT)*: a sound-responsive, mood-based lighting fixture, targeting college students and youth. Our current prototype reacts to volume levels by changing light intensity, using programmable LED strips and a six-bar tensegrity structure. In the future, we hope to incorporate additional features such as (1) Microcontrollers that change the color of light in response to music and (2) Making the lights move using motors, springs, real-time motion control and rods that can expand and contract in response to music, user commands and other external stimuli. We believe this product addresses a large market, particularly (1) Entertainment venues and events like music festivals, concerts and exhibitions and (2) Home furniture and decorative, multifunctional lights. Here's a video (http://tinyurl.com/mbzcsfl) showing our product in action!*

Patrick Angelo
B.S. Mechanical Engineering, 2018

Jocelyn Kim
B.S. Chemical Engineering, 2018

Vineet Nair
B.S. Mechanical Engineering and Economics, 2018

Nicole Parker
B.S. Mechanical Engineering, 2017

Alvin Tan
B.S. Mechanical Engineering, 2018

Faculty Mentor: Euiyoung Kim, Jacobs Institute for Design Innovation

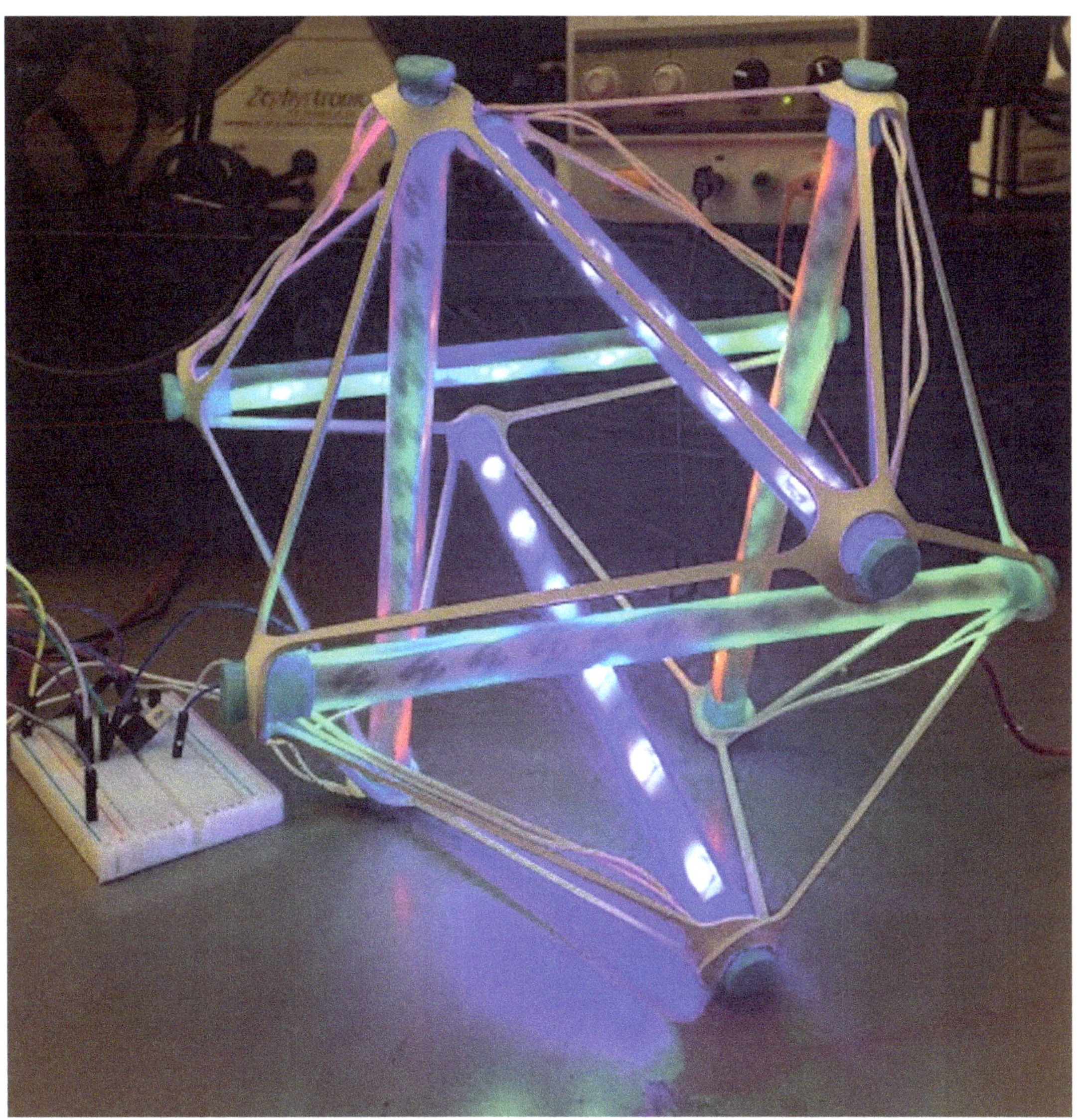

Patrick Angelo, Jocelyn Kim, Vineet Nair, Nicole Parker, Alvin Tan, *Lights in Tensegrity (LiT)*, 2017.
Lasercut rubber lattice and 3D printed end caps, programmable LEDs and electronics, 12 x 12 x 12 inches.

WheelSense

For the 10 percent of those who use a wheelchair, independent travel is nearly impossible. Users are wary of "self-driving" wheelchairs that reduce their control and can only operate in limited environments. One such person, Tomás and Corten's friend Daniel, has both cerebral palsy and cortical vision impairment. His greatest challenge is navigating new places. He has fallen down ramps multiple times and often collides with objects even at home. Tomás organized some friends for a week-long "make-a-thon" at Daniel's house in Los Gatos, Calif., to identify his daily challenges and come up with practical ways to prevent injury and promote independence. After deciding that better navigation would have the greatest impact, the group hacked Daniel's wheelchair to add ramp lateral-edge detection, frontal drop-off detection, and backup assistance through auditory and haptic feedback. The chair sounds one tone when it detects a frontal drop-off such as stairs or a curb, and a different tone when it detects an obstacle while the chair is moving in reverse, and it vibrates the appropriate armrest when a wheel gets too close to the edge of a ramp. The resulting WheelSense chair that uses this novel feedback approach represents a breakthrough because it allows Daniel to remain completely in control, making independent travel more realistic. Following the make-a-thon, Tomás left the prototype with Daniel for further evaluation under the supervision of Daniel's older brother. After a couple of weeks, some of the chair's sensor mounts broke off, demonstrating the need for improvements. The wheelchair was sent to Berkeley, where Tomás recruited Corten to make WheelSense more robust. Corten developed stronger sensor mounts capable of withstanding frequent use and multiple bumps into obstacles.

Tomas Vega Galvez
B.A. Computer Science
and Cognitive Science, 2017

Corten Singer Winger
B.A. Computer Science
and Cognitive Science, 2017

Faculty Mentors: Edward Lee, EECS, and
Björn Hartmann, EECS and Jacobs Institute for Design Innovation

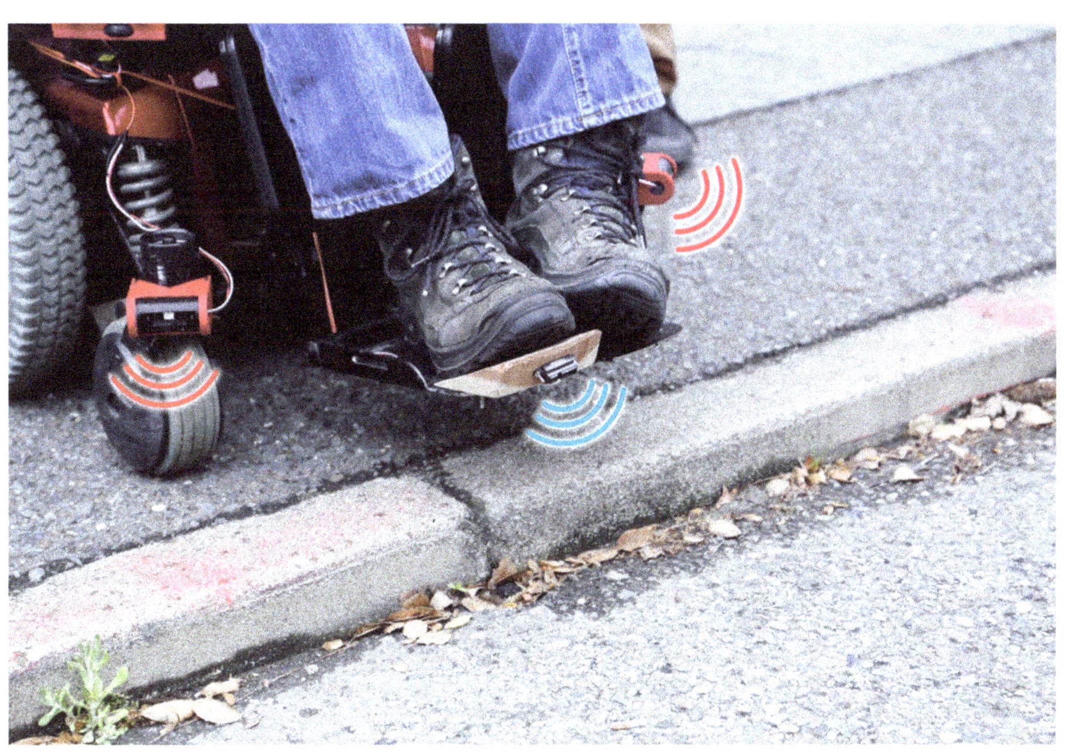

Tomas Vega Galvez, Corten Singer Winger, *WheelSense*, 2016. Assistive technology.

Arvin Tanu

Dual Identity *is a four-weeks-long architectural project which explores the possibility of form to accommodate function, adapting the 'outside-in' design process. The project is located on Bancroft Way, Berkeley, and built on top of the existing old dancing studio.* Dual Identity *responds to both rigid and static characters of the surrounding buildings, while addressing the dynamic rhythm of dancing through aesthetic body performances. Hence, this duality creates contrast composition between the "Blob" (public area) and the "Box" (dancing studio). The two entities dance to compliment each other in redefining the dancing studio area, while maintaining visual compliments for the public audiences and the dancers.*

Arvin Tanu
B.A. Architecture, 2017
Circus Student Winner, 2017

Faculty Mentor: Jean Paul-Bourdier, College of Environmental Design

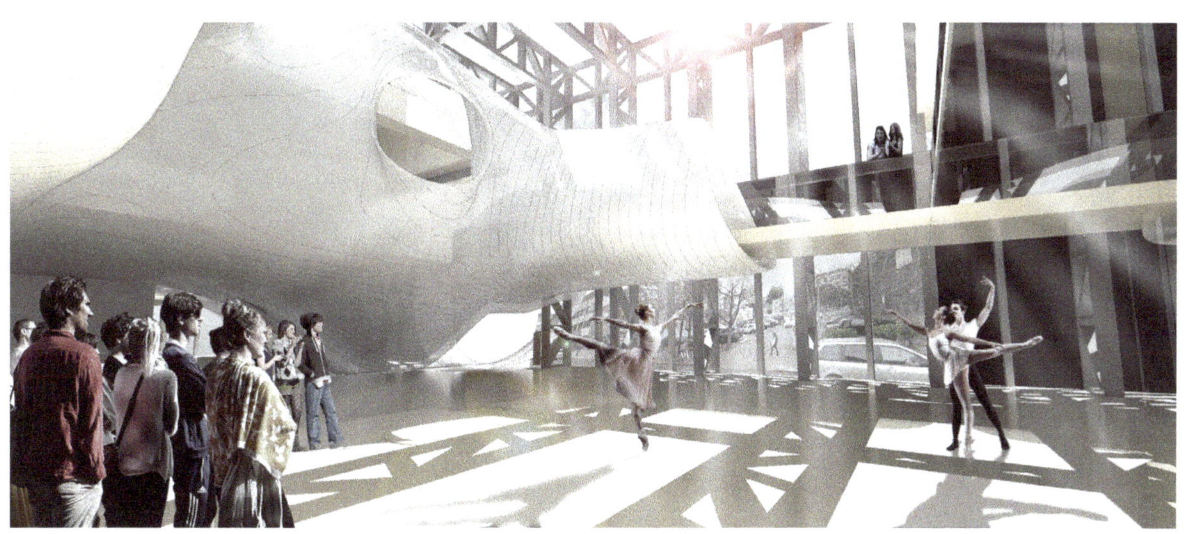

Arvin Tanu, *Dual Identity*, 2016. Museum board, 40 x 32 inches.

Kristen Wilson

"The Surveillance of the Screen" argues that twentieth century cinema's increasing awareness of itself as a medium of potential exploitation (of unlicensed watching) as well as a medium with fluctuating power relations between director and audience allows three masters of twentieth century cinema to explore and ultimately work through the visual and theoretical implications of exploitative and therefore immoral watching. In Fritz Lang's Metropolis, *Charlie Chaplin's* Modern Times, *and Stanley Kubrick's* A Clockwork Orange, *the relationship between director and audience, between watching and being watched in turn, is dramatically renegotiated as each director engages in meta commentary regarding what the new medium of cinema should be and what purposes it (as well as the audience and director) should be expected to fulfill.*

Kristen Wilson
B.A. English and American Studies, 2017
Chauncey Wetmore Wells Critical Essay Prize, 2017

Faculty Mentors: George Starr, English

The Surveillance of the Screen

Scopophilia, or the love of looking, foregrounds the very foundations of filmmaking. The relationship of surveillance to film, of screens to surveillers, has always been a central issue of concern for the film industry—who is watching who, how are they watching, and what power does that watching afford them? As our understandings of screens, surveillance, and film have evolved, new power differentials have made themselves apparent, the authority that screens (and therefore surveillance) offer expanded outwards from elites to the masses with less than utopian results across time, both in diegetic and non-diegetic understandings of this expansion. However, Stanley Kubrick's *A Clockwork Orange* (1971) challenged the growing sophistication of audiences of its day, subverting several film conventions and subsequently reopening the discussion on the morality of surveillance and therefore film, particularly as a means of entertainment and therefore pleasure.

From the first frame—a bolt of red that blinds the watcher sitting in a dark room—Kubrick's *A Clockwork Orange* seeks to unnerve and unbalance the viewer, depriving them of the watcher's authority that well-versed film audiences of the 1970s could claim as seasoned filmgoers. Instead, Kubrick reclaims the authority of the director by producing something deeply uncomfortable and often downright unpleasant to watch, a horror movie that depicts the terrible punishment of not being able to look away from the screen. Alex, the authoritative watcher and primary exhibitionist throughout the film, punctuates his horrible realization of his punishment with the words, "But I could not shut me glassies. And even if I tried to move my glassballs about, I still could not get out of the line of fire of this picture" (*A Clockwork Orange*, 1:13:40). His sudden understanding of the film as something dangerous, something fearful that is causing him harm, something which he cannot escape the "line of fire" of is precisely the realization that Kubrick wants his audience to have as they watch his film. The scientists in the back of the room, the ones who have presumably cut together the film and prepared Alex to watch it, are in fact practicing the greatest wish of many a director: to affect a watcher so deeply with emotion that a film becomes more than just a carrier for human thought and plot, but for unbearable human emotion as well. Kubrick takes this aspiration to its dark extreme, he himself represented in some sense by the scientists in the back of the room—*A Clockwork Orange* means to trap the watcher, to make it impossible for them to look away from the unsettling and often disgusting display of human vileness before their eyes.

Alex, as a character and narrator, is immediately remarkable for how unlikeable he is. He suffers from no empathy or even sympathy for his fellow man and certainly has no respect for human life, property, or justice. The fact that the audience is situated with such a figure is completely counter to usual constructions of narrative in which the audience follows someone they can root for; in this film, it is safe to say that exceedingly few people are rooting for Alex to continue to rape and pillage without consequence. Kubrick's choice to maintain the book's close, oppressive contact with its vile narrator has the effect of trapping the audience into a state of powerlessness, much like Alex strapped into his chair. Even if one chooses to root against Alex, there is little fulfillment in watching him get what is coming to him, and even this fulfillment is later spoiled as the film dredges up deeper concerns of free will and morality on a societal scale that cannot be answered by merely hating Alex.

Perhaps even more interesting than Alex's fundamental unlikeability, Kubrick also goes out of his way to position Alex as an authoritative watcher as well as an exhibitionist. Kubrick accomplishes this by using his opening credit sequence to unsettle audiences from their comfortable positions as watchers, opening up that position for Alex. The sheer physical experience of the incredibly saturated red washing over an audience after a period of blackness not only makes it momentarily difficult to look at the screen, but also *illuminates* the audience, ruining the otherwise safe isolation one has from both events on the screen and fellow watchers in the theater. Further, Kubrick does not allow for his audience to grow used to the red background, switching to blue as soon as their eyes begin to adjust, and then back to red again—the watcher is never given the chance to be fully comfortable with what they are seeing, and therefore has none of their usual mastery over and distance from what is depicted on-screen.

It is from this position of utter disempowerment as watchers—simultaneously blinded and illuminated by solid blocks of color that offer little to actually see—that the audience is given a close-up of Alex, unblinking and staring directing into the camera, at each individual audience member. After an uncomfortably long period of time (more than fifteen seconds), the shot zooms out to reveal two of Alex's droogs, but Alex is the only one wearing eyeballs (which may or may not be faux) as cufflinks. In this, there seems both the thread of the authoritative watcher, Alex staring unblinkingly at the audience and wearing eyes for cufflinks, and the exhibitionist, aware that he is being watched and performing to that end, raising a glass of milk slowly to reveal his cufflinks to the audience, perhaps the eyes of the last person who dared to watch him. The effect of the camera zooming out begins to feel like a retreat, the audience eager to escape from Alex's malevolent gaze and the implications therein. The camera retreats for a full forty seconds before Alex makes a godlike interjection, narrating over the diegetic world and claiming this story, this film, as his own, becoming more than a mere character oblivious to those watching him. No, Alex is fully aware that he has an audience, and the first thing he tells them reveals both his consent to be watched (exhibitionist) and a sense that a future version of himself is watching as well (authoritative watcher): "There was me" (ACO 1:40).

The camera frequently reinforces Alex's position as both authoritative watcher and exhibitionist, focusing on him for several seconds at a time before than giving a reverse shot at what he is looking at, the violence of his gaze predicting future acts of destruction against the object of his attention, these acts of destruction then exhibited before the audience. Alex's position as both authoritative watcher and exhibitionist is even further unique in a society without apparent mass surveillance, as exists in many other dystopias. In Alex's society, the fear is not in being watched, but in being made to watch, the entire movie an exercise in exposing the audience to the discomfort and revulsion of watching as several scenes in the film manifest specific horrors related to watching. There are, of course, Alex's turns in the straightjacket and chair, being made to watch filmed horrors and have a negative reaction to them, but there are also the perspectives of Alex's victims, both the elderly writer who is made to watch his wife's rape and the cat lady who is made to watch the penis sculpture descend upon her, crushing her and killing her. In these scenes, Kubrick takes care to position the camera both so the audience can see the horrified reactions of the victims as well as the crime from the victims' point of view, the audience experiencing such horror themselves as they watch the crime happen directly, as if a crime visited against each individual member of the audience. Before Alex rapes the writer's wife, he speaks into the camera (to the writer and audience) and says: "Viddy well, little brother, viddy well!" (ACO 13:10), again an invitation to watch the horror as it unfolds, as Alex commits it. This is Alex the exhibitionist, invested in making sure that people are watching him at all times, at all costs, his victims (especially the writer) restrained and helpless not to watch.

In a key moment of disempowerment, Alex's position as authoritative watcher is taken from him when his droogs break a milk bottle against his face, blinding him and leaving him to be arrested by the police. From thereon, the camera begins to treat Alex very differently, authority figures pictured looking down on him, Alex held in the power of their gaze, and the power and validity of Alex's sight constantly being called into question. In one key instance, he tries to convince the scientists to stop his treatment, calling out to them, "I've learned my lesson, sir! I see now what I've never seen before! I'm cured, praise God!" (ACO 1:18:40). To which the scientists refuse to believe that he has really learned his lesson, proceeding almost as if Alex is an unsophisticated viewer of film who must be taught to watch film "correctly," this a horror that the audience may well identify with. Soon after Alex is deprived of his authoritative watching, Alex's exhibitionism is taken from him as well, placed on a stage before government and law enforcement officials and then unable to act out any of the violent intent that motivated his exhibitionism previously, instead falling terribly ill when he tries to do so.

The horror in depriving Alex of his authoritative watching and exhibitionism is not only the deprivation of free will that inevitably follows, but even more importantly the very same horror as is on display throughout the rest of the film: the horror of not being able to look away. The screen, and the silent film that Alex is made to watch on that screen, becomes a device of reformation, a remaking of the self through self-surveillance. Alex's manufactured conscience becomes the authoritative watcher, ready and willing to punish him for any violence he sees rather than just the violence he intends to commit. Again, sight is privileged even over intention; seeing is believing and intention is fickle and more difficult to parse out, intention as given to nuance as language is and therefore untrustworthy in a visual medium. The final scene of the film, of Alex in the hospital having his picture taken with a minister by a dozen photographers, sees him returned to his old position of control, freed from the effects of his treatment and able to take on the roles of exhibitionist and authoritative watcher once more. It is difficult to imagine a happy ending for this film, but it is perhaps even more difficult to stomach that Kubrick has returned us, the audience, to exactly the position we originated from, enduring this trial of watching a series of horrors for little appreciable change in Alex's character or the world he inhabits, exercising the director's ultimate control over the audience's watching and pleasure taken from that watching.

Kristen Wilson, *The Surveillance of the Screen*.
Excerpt from research paper, 19 pages, 2016.

Mollie Sitzer

Remembering the desert night sky in Palm Springs, I wanted to create hotel spaces for each room that drew people outside when dusk comes to experience the beauty of the stars.

Mollie Sitzer
B.A. Landscape Architecture, 2016
Circus Student Winner, 2017

Faculty Mentor: Chip Sullivan, College of Environmental Design

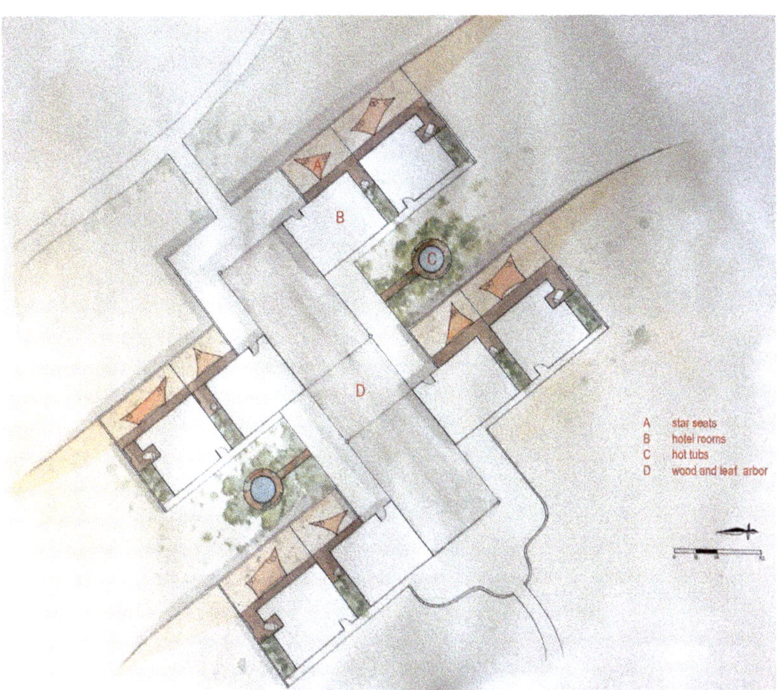

Mollie Sitzer, *Star Seats*, 2017. Watercolor on bristol, 4 x 6 feet.

IDENTITIES AND TRANSITIONS

GABRIEL CAZARES
WHITEWASHING MACHINE
REPLIKA
MADELINE KRESIN
REEMPLOY
MOIRA LABAND
IRENE CHEN
SAHVANNA MAZON

Gabriel Cazares

Relationships. Career. Money. Some things sound too good to turn down. After being denied from college, Miguel Martín encounters strange people who hope to influence his path in life. He must decide on whether or not to abandon a dream for what appears to be a newfound opportunity.

Artistic contributors include:
Irene Chen
Regina Pigsley
Aurora Jimenez

Gabriel Cazares
B.A. Film and Media Studies, 2017

Faculty Mentor: J. Mira Kopell, Film & Media

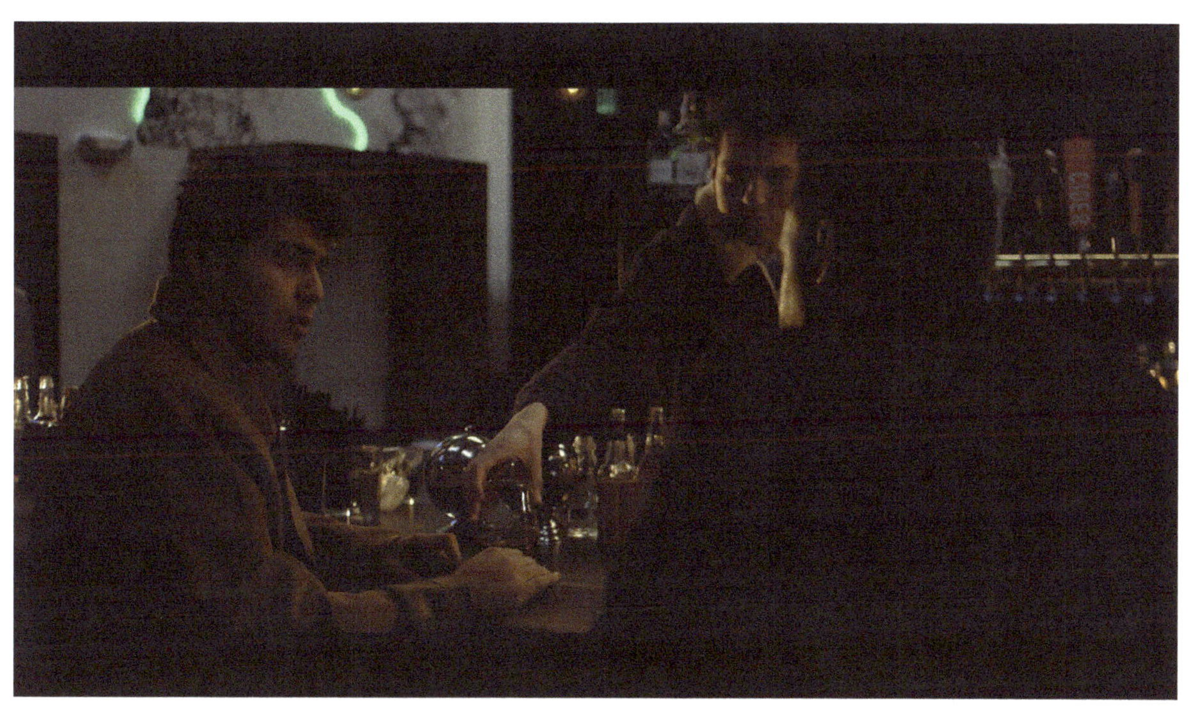

Gabriel Cazares, *Years from Now*, 2017. Color, digital video, 14 minutes.

Whitewashing Machine

Our whitewashing machine takes in an Asian character from Asian-inspired storylines and whitewashes it accordingly. It operates using your average Hollywood business executive who aims to increase profits with the misconception that Asians are not popular enough to star in major movie roles.

Our goal was to bring attention to the explicit absurdity of whitewashing and the white savior narrative that plagues Hollywood, theater, and popular media. Both our performance art piece and its complementary infomercial serve as satirical devices that raise awareness of the erasure and mis-portrayal of Asian and Asian-American identities in media and its normalization. Introducing our product to the university environment, particularly the laundry rooms of freshmen dorms, our washing machine-like device plays on the typical first year college student narrative of not knowing how to do laundry but being expected to. We hope our design and performance serve as a call to action to the younger generation of college students to view racial bias in the media similarly to their first-time laundry doing dilemma—a problem that many are confronting for the first time but one that nonetheless should be solved.

Patrick Burden
B.S. Business Administration, 2017

Carlo Liquido
M.S. Information and Management Systems, 2017

Danielle Kenwood
B.A. Cognitive Science, 2017

Isabel Wang
B.A. Architecture, 2018

Alex Sung
B.A. Computer Science, 2017

Faculty Mentor: Jill Miller, Berkeley Center for New Media

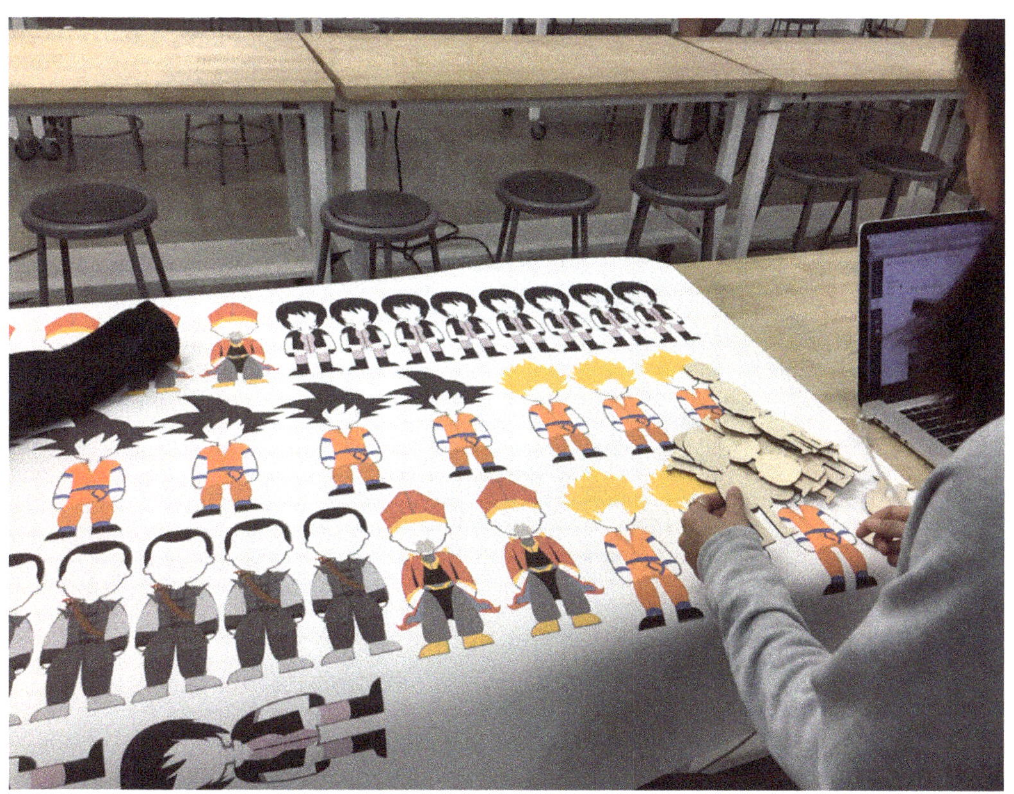

Patrick Burden, Danielle Kenwood, Carlo Liquido, Alex Sung, Isabel Wang, *Whitewashing Machine*, 2016.
Live performance, laser cut wood, electronics, sticker printing.

Replika

How close is humanity getting to replicating human consciousness & simulating circuits that act like neurons? This is the question we're being thrown into on a daily basis as we come closer & closer to creating algorithms capable of generating intelligent & self-aware responses. How soon will these digital minds surpass the Turing test? Integrating artificial intelligence is a near reality in modern life, as rapidly occurring implementation makes its path clearer. It's up to our own volition in 2017 to decide how we will allow these "others" to be a part of our lives. From online chatbots to smart algorithms to voice responsive systems, robotic forms breach the uncanny valley, & even cinema. AI is taking the forms of everything from enemy, companion, lover, servant, & more. Our project seeks to question the place of AI in the future where human-ness & artificial thought are blurred & transmuted. Human connection is amended, thoughts & feelings are traversed, & roles in society are questioned.

Patrick Burden
B.A. Business Administration, 2017

Sebastian Ospina
B.A. Cognitive Science, 2017

Miranda Clemmons
B.A. Cognitive Science, 2017

Shota Pangilinan
B.A. Cognitive Science, 2017

Faculty Mentors: James Pierce, Jacobs Institute for Design Innovation

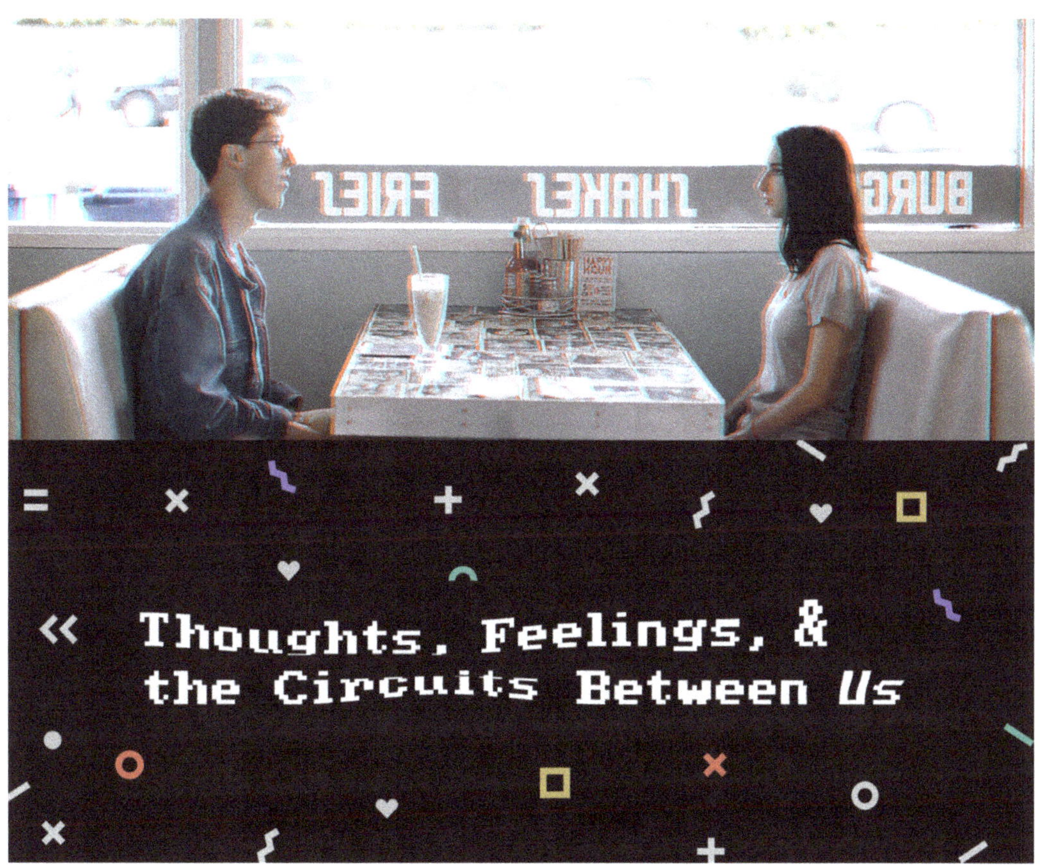

Patrick Burden, Miranda Clemmons, Sebastian Ospina, Shota Pangilinan, *Replika*, 2017.
Digital interface, speculative design.

Madeline Kresin

In this essay, I analyze Jane Austen's depiction of Henrietta Bates as an anti-self to the heroine, Emma, and to Austenian style itself. Emma *is a novel split between a single consciousness (Emma's free indirect discourse) and the quotidian events of the outside world. Miss Bates exists as both a challenge to the disembodied narratorial voice's drive toward abstraction and absolute truth, and to Emma's conception of herself as a particular being superior to the rest of the world.*

Madeline Kresin
B.A. English, 2018
Chauncey Wetmore Wells Critical Essay Prize, 2017

Faculty Mentor: David A. Miller, English

Solicitude for Shoes: Henrietta Bates in Emma

Jane Austen's *Emma* is built upon the dialectic of a single, unfolding consciousness juxtaposed with the unknown expanse of the external world. Austen intertwines her introduction of this consciousness with the introduction of the novel: "Emma Woodhouse, handsome, clever, and rich, with a comfortable home and happy disposition, seemed to unite some of the best blessings of existence; and had lived nearly twenty-one years in the world with very little to distress or vex her." (5) Immediately, we see the dangerous permeability of the division between individuality and isolation; the "world" in which Emma Woodhouse has "lived nearly twenty-one years" is composed of a "comfortable home and happy disposition". Against this image of particularity and narratorial preference (as in the textual balancing of Emma's free indirect discourse and the narrative voice), Austen positions the figure of Miss Bates as simultaneously isolated in her single status (the "poor old maid") and fully belonging to this public outside world which Emma cannot quite comprehend.

Miss Bates is continually posed as an exception to the general rule. Despite her lack of all that Emma possesses, Miss Bates wondrously enjoys a "most uncommon degree of popularity." In contrast, Emma thinks of "[the] warmth and tenderness of heart ... which makes [Mr. Woodhouse] so dearly beloved ... [and] gives Isabella all her *popularity*" (269, emphasis added) and realizes, "I have it not." There is something verging on pathos in Emma's acknowledgment of her lack of "warmth and tenderness of heart," so that in the very narratorial privilege of Emma's consciousness, Austen plants the seed of isolation. Herein we see another iteration of Austen's preoccupation with balance in narrative. In the relation between Emma and Miss Bates we see a working-through of excess and lack, singularity and plurality, toward some greater whole, the "perfect happiness of the union" (484) that admits no fragmentation. Thus the conclusion of the novel excises Miss Bates from the narrative entirely. It is as if Emma, to be made whole, needs not only to marry Mr. Knightley (and thus move from singular to coupled), but to remove or subsume Henrietta Bates.

While Emma begins the novel as a definitive particular—we move from the title page inscribed *Emma* to the first word, "Emma"—Miss Bates brings with her the outside world. Austen writes, "Her youth had passed without distinction, and her middle of life was devoted to the care of a failing mother, and the endeavour to make a small income go as far as possible. And yet she was a happy woman, and a woman whom no one named without good-will. It was her own *universal* good-will and contented temper which worked such wonders. She loved *every* body, was interested in *every* body's happiness, quick-sighted to *every* body's merits; thought herself a most fortunate creature, and surrounded with blessings in such an excellent mother and *so many* good neighbours and friends, and a home that wanted for nothing. The simplicity and cheerfulness of her nature, her contented and grateful spirit, were a recommendation to *every* body and a mine of felicity to herself." (21, emphasis added) While Emma's world is confined precisely to Hartfield, marked by ventures to the outside world of Highbury (the Crown, Randalls, and Donwell Abbey, with one extraordinary jaunt to Box Hill), Miss Bates belongs to a more generalized world of "universal" and "every body." Miss Bates' popularity, like her volubility, is seemingly infinite: her kindness works "*wonders*," introducing the element of the miraculous to this quotidian, delineated world. However, even as Miss Bates compels the narrative to reveal a more expansive vocabulary and population, she inevitably is brought back to a position of isolation. The sentence ends not with the "recommendation to every body" but the "mine of felicity to herself," implying a kind of hollow, bottomless darkness. Austen differentiates Emma's "comfortable home" with Miss Bates' "home that wanted for nothing;" while both are self-sufficient, Miss Bates' sufficiency is determined by a negation of the possibility she could be allowed to want. It is an enforced, rather than "comfortable" totality.

Miss Bates' continual position as relational to other characters allows her to simultaneously embody the social, public world and the frightening image of solitude. It is always "Miss Bates and ..." There is a particular cruelty in the connection Austen draws between Miss Bates and her niece, Jane Fairfax. Although Austen makes more transparent the unhappy discrepancy between Emma and Jane, ("Mr Knightley had once told [Emma] that [Emma's dislike of Jane] was because she saw in her the really accomplished young woman, which she wanted to be thought herself" (166)), Austen also poses Jane as a kind of holy ideal for Miss Bates, one by which she finds definition and purpose. In Jane Fairfax, "there, not to be vulgar, [is] *distinction*, and merit." (167, emphasis added) By figuring the connection through Emma's free indirect discourse rather than direct, authorial narration, Austen avoids the "vulgarity" of an exact comparison between Miss Bates' lack and Jane's absolute possession. When Miss Bates is not named as the Miss among two other married women, she is either the "aunt" or joined to Jane Fairfax's name with an "and." Austen manages to simultaneously deposit Miss Bates into the multiplicity, the world of others against Emma's particularized consciousness, and mark Miss Bates' difference from this multiplicity as crucially lacking some characteristic everyone else shares. For much of the novel, Miss Bates, like *Sense and Sensibility*'s Elinor Dashwood, "suffer[s] the punishments of an attachment, without enjoying its advantages" (264).

However, Austen does not allow for Miss Bates to be made ridiculous in a state of eternal suffering. Miss Bates is, without equivocation, a "happy woman". Her happiness, like her wondrous kindness and externalizing interest in others, has the ability to overwhelm all the supposed rules of poverty and despair. In the phrase "happy woman", there is something definite, admitting no vagarity or multiplicity. In contrast, Austen writes that Emma is in possession of a "happy disposition" (5). "Happy disposition" revels in ambiguity: is Emma disposed to be happy (a potential state) or is her character defined by its ability to be happy (an absolute state)? Miss Bates has somehow achieved this state of happiness to which Emma spends the novel striving.

Austen juxtaposes Emma's conception of herself as composed of a kind of wholeness and integrity, indeed all-sufficiency, with the portrayal of Miss Bates' fragmentary, incomplete self. When Harriet, astonished that Emma does not wish to marry, exclaims, "'But then, to be an old maid at last, like Miss Bates!'", Emma replies "'That is as formidable an image as you could present, Harriet; and if I thought I should ever be like Miss Bates! so silly—so satisfied—so smiling—so prosing—so undistinguishing and unfastidious—and so apt to tell every thing relative to every body about me, I would marry to-morrow. But between *us*, I am convinced there never can be any likeness, except in being unmarried." (84–85) Harriet's "at last" indicates that Miss Bates' status as an "old maid" is a kind of ultimate, a horizon they are ever approaching, so that the text is infused with an (albeit ironic) urgency to not become Miss Bates. Although Emma will soon remark, "nobody is afraid of [Miss Bates]: that is a great charm" (85), we can already see that the figure of Miss Bates wields a fearsome power over Emma. Bharat Tandon writes that "one reason Emma Woodhouse is so troubled by Miss Bates is that she can divine in the spinster's glossolalia something of herself, or of what she herself might one day become"[1].

It is not just Emma but the text itself which seems to "divine" and insist upon this fear of the communion between Emma and Miss Bates. Emma repeats and doubles the narratorial encapsulation of herself in a triplet, so that we move from "handsome, clever and rich" to the expansive, even ineloquent "so silly—so satisfied—so smiling—so prosing—so undistinguishing and unfastidious—and so apt to tell every thing relative to every body about me." Emma's contempt (and subconscious horror) at Harriet's suggestion is registered as a shock and degradation to language itself. Austen moves from the pleasant alliteration of the first triplet to an increasingly expansive and unruled second triplet; the progression of Emma's anger reveals an eerie similarity to Miss Bates' own patterns of speech. Crucially, Emma stretches the conclusion of the phrase "and if I thought I should ever be like Miss Bates!" to the point of senselessness. (In the sheer length of the middle qualitative phrase, it is easy to forget the preceding clause.)

In her incredulity at Harriet's suggestion of an equivalence between Emma and Miss Bates, Emma prefigures Miss Bates' interminable style of never finishing a thought or phrase. Furthermore, the dashes separating each phrase mimic the speaker's breathing, so that instead of a refined and unbodied voice, there is a clear marking of Emma's physicality. As will become apparent, Miss Bates' speech registers a transformation from the abstract to the concrete, creating not an aloof elegance but a visceral reality. It is as if the very suggestion of Miss Bates is enough to momentarily solidify Emma, and make her as dependent on the needs of the body as Isabella, Mr. Woodhouse, or even Mrs. Bates.

Miss Bates exists as a kind of doubling, or anti-self, of Emma, not just in her manipulative prowess to order and ensure the stability of her world and her position in it, but also in her narrative mastery. Emma, desperate to distract Harriet from the topic of Mr. Elton, calls upon Miss and Mrs. Bates to "seek safety in numbers". (155) In Emma's free indirect discourse (the textual embodiment of her consciousness), Miss Bates here represents the "generous public" (85), the multiplicity that further ensures Emma's own particularity. However, once Miss Bates is presented in the diegetic world, in the same room as Emma and her consciousness, we see a reworking of Miss Bates' indeterminate status. Austen writes that Emma and Harriet are "gratefully" welcomed by Mrs. Bates and "her more active, talking daughter, almost ready to overpower them with care and kindness, thanks for their visit, solicitude for their shoes, anxious inquiries after Mr. Woodhouse's health, cheerful communications about her mother's, and sweet-cake from the beaufet ..." (156)

Just as Harriet's equivalence of Miss Bates to Emma forces Emma to reveal a more bodily presence in her voice (as the dashes represent short breaths), here too Miss Bates, even in a narratorial summary of her speech, introduces a more minute and physical image. The aloof and distant "thanks for their visit" is immediately followed by "solicitude for their shoes," so that the reader is made to realize they are all, in fact, wearing shoes. Rather than the disembodied authorial voice and the vaguely bodied consciousness, Miss Bates' "overpowering kindness" insists upon a grounded, physical reality in which all of the characters are fully people rather than flattened types.

Herein arises the problem of morality in *Emma*. It is no longer possible to dismiss the narratorial cruelty toward minor characters (such as Miss Bates and her mother). As unembodied, social representations, (Emma's portrait of the generalized poor old maid), a character may be mocked without any stirrings of conscience in Emma or the reader. However, Miss Bates renders the world around her as fully real (when she discusses their shoes, the characters are literally grounded in the quotidian world), forcing the reader to view the characters not as abstractions but as people. Thus Miss Bates exposes the immorality of Emma's (and the narrator's) sophisticated mockery. Miss Bates' narratorial function is one of expansion as well as actualization; she introduces the reader to the details of ordinary life, both private (shoes) and public (the household duties of Mrs. Cole), above which Emma's consciousness floats.

Miss Bates' last appearance in the novel occurs as a narratorial abstraction. Crucially, Austen ties the news of Mrs. Weston's baby (the continuance of life) to Miss Bates' power of spreading news, rhyming Emma's early depiction of the single woman with a narrow income as the sport of boys and girls. Austen writes, "[Mr Weston] must tell [Emma]; and Miss Bates being present, it passed, of course, to Mrs. Cole, Mrs. Perry, and Mrs. Elton, immediately afterwards." (468) We see yet another incarnation of the triplet, yet this time Miss Bates is held apart from its inevitable consonance. Although Miss Bates has retreated from a speaking role to a matter-of-fact presence, "Miss Bates being present," her ability to talk is revealed as that which connects the joyous news of the particular to the social. Like the novel itself, Miss Bates is "a great talker upon little matters." (21) It is easy for the reader to skim over her inane diatribes about pork shoulders, apples, and Mrs. Cole's household vagaries. However, it is through these diatribes that the reader is given a glimpse at "all those little matters on which the daily happiness of private life depends." (117)

Madeline Kresin, *Solicitude for Shoes: Henrietta Bates in Jane Austen's* Emma.
Excerpt from research paper, 14 pages, 2017.

ReEmploy

When refugees come to a new country, they are faced with the daunting task of finding secure employment, on top of learning a new language and creating a new home for themselves. Being unable to find employment may lead to social and cultural isolation as well as long-term feelings of hopelessness and rejection that may then spiral into extremism as an alternative escape. Here comes ReEmploy, *a refugee networking platform for refugees to find local tasks as a means of building and expanding their local network for resettlement and community engagement.* ReEmploy *features real-time language translation, Humans of New York style refugee profiles, and a reviews system to ensure accountability.*

Serena Chang
B.S. Electrical Engineering
and Computer Science, 2017

Michael Chen
B.A. Computer Science, 2017

Nikhil Patel
B.A. Computer Science, 2018

Audrey Tsai
B.A. Cognitive Science
and Computer Science, 2017

Faculty Mentors: Bjorn Hartmann and Zvika Krieger,
Jacobs Institute for Design Innovation

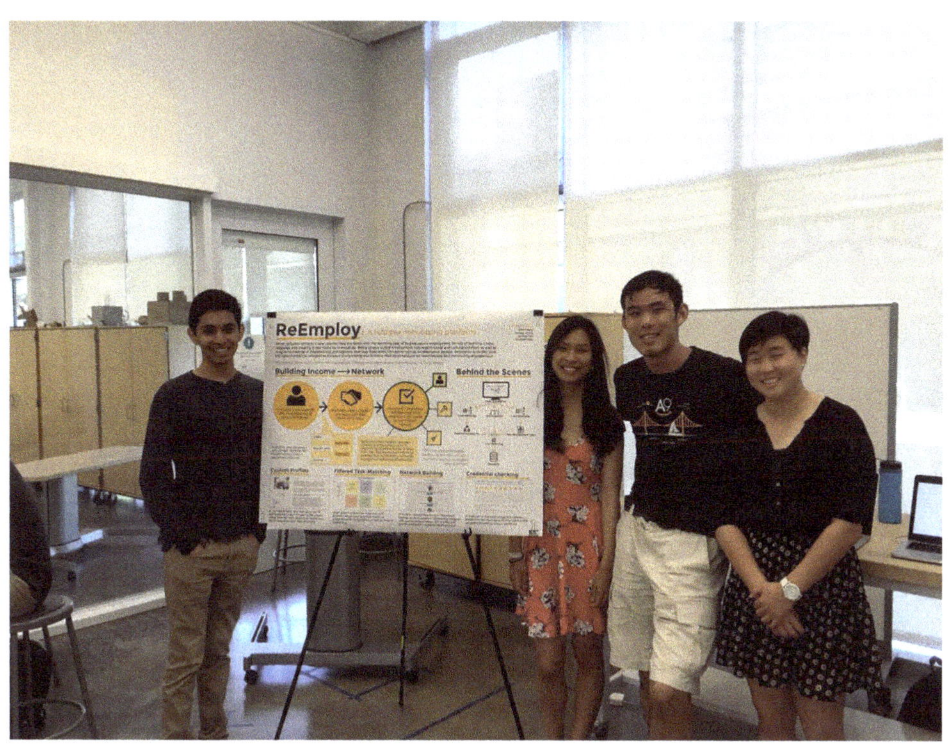

Serena Chang, Michael Chen, Nikhil Patel, Audrey Tsai, *ReEmploy*, 2017.

Moira Laband

A dark yet comical take on the harsh reality of the "white picket fence" family. In this film, what was once the epitome of the perfect American family deteriorates as a result of broken trust. After obsessing over footage of her husband cheating on her, Trish engages in absurd actions of sabotage. However, her attempts continuously backfire, each time damaging or ripping a piece of her clothing until she is left naked and vulnerable. Ultimately, this film plays on the literal, exaggerated externalization of the protagonist's internal state of mind—a state of jealousy, obsession, and chaos. On the surface, the couple in the film may just be hitting a road bump, however the emotional weight of the film comes when we realize the conflict extends much farther than this particular point in the characters' lives. The attention subtly shifts to the fate of the child, and what his parents are arguing about hardly matters anymore. The damage has been, and still is, being done. Although children may seem innocent and unaware, the early stages in life are critical for healthy psychological development, and parents are the primary influencers. The comical spin on this more serious topic is a view on life that I personally want to have more of—to be able to find humor in hardship.

Moira Laband
B.A. Film and Media Studies and Psychology, 2017

Faculty Mentor: J. Mira Koppell, Film and Media Studies

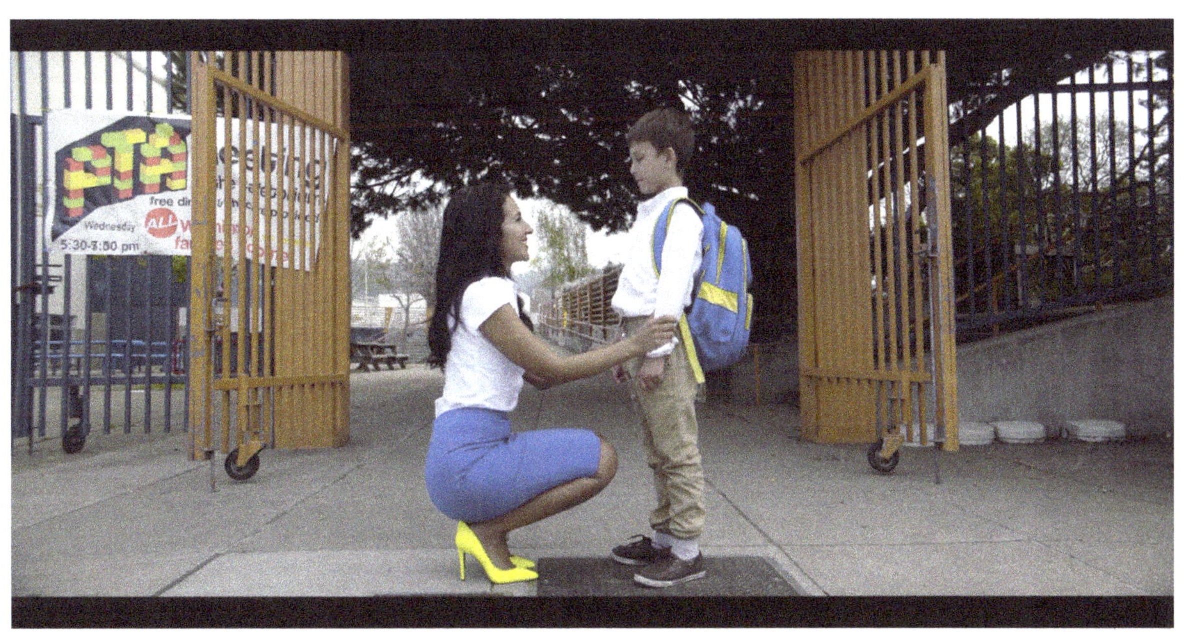

Moira Laband, *Striptease*, 2017. Short film, 11:18 minutes.

Irene Chen

Expecting *is a short film about a young woman, Renee, who struggles to leave an abusive relationship. Though it is a difficult choice for her to make, she decides to run away and stays at her sister's home for the sake of her unborn child, of which her husband has no knowledge of.*

But the psychological consequences of her husband's abuse follow her beyond physical distance. She steps out of her sister's home one day into the public space and realizes that across the street, in front of her, and behind her— he's everywhere.

Renee continues to stay in her sister's home. One morning as she and her sister are asleep in bed, the door knocks. Her sister answers. Just a student looking for some signatures for a cause. Her sister closes the door. The door knocks again— and Renee hears his voice. And only after this incident does Renee discover the strength of her own will to survive.

Irene Chen
B.A. Art Practice, Rhetoric, Film Studies, 2017
Eisner Prize, 2017

Faculty Mentors: J. Mira Koppell, Film & Media

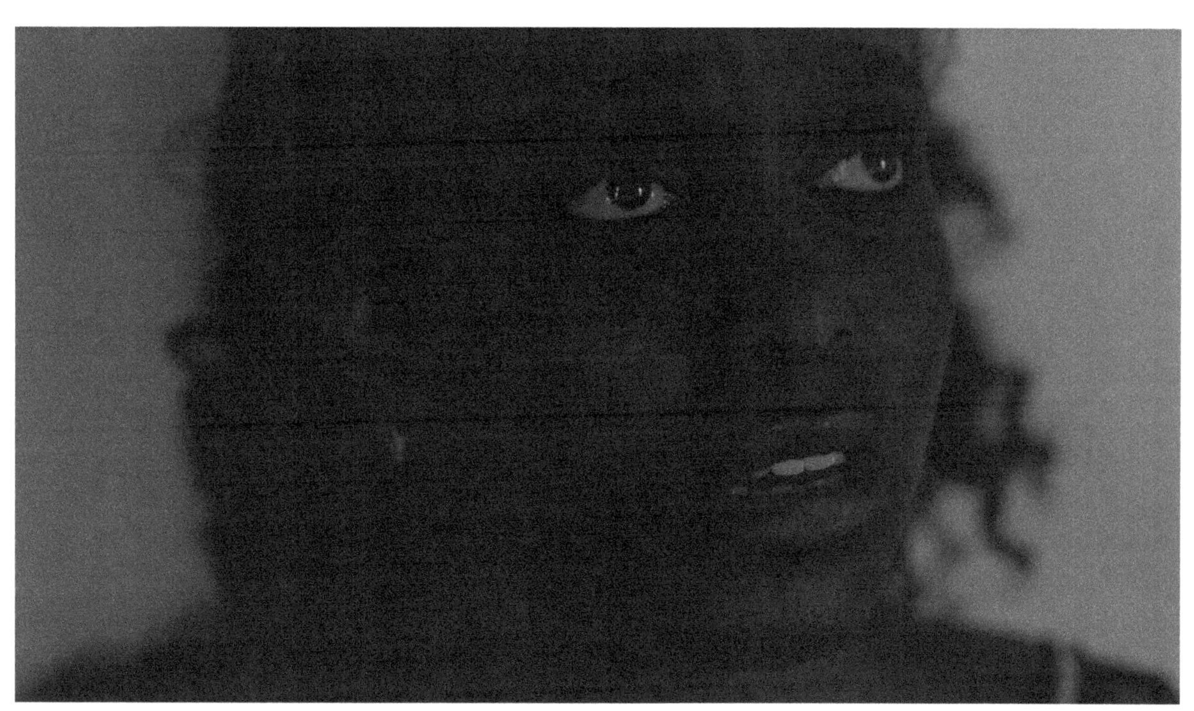

Irene Chen, *Expecting*, 2016. Video, 9:18 minutes.

Sahvanna Mazon

Watercolored self is a collection of poetry that reflects on how the individual views themselves in relation to others. This is done by reflecting on color, specifically in the ways that it effects perception. The poetry itself is an experimentation of several forms—with the primary being the ghazal, which weaves and morphs throughout the collection—ultimately creating a diverse arrangement of writing.

Sahvanna Mazon
B.A. English, 2017
Roselyn Schneider Eisner Poetry Prize, 2017

Faculty Mentors: Ken Mahru and Lyn Hejinian, English

Palette 2

You are lucky they said, your skin
so pale and pure looks good in red.

Hiding in books to avoid mundane life
you developed a mixed identity, but are well red.

Just a hint of blush, the shade
when cast, might smudge a little too red.

Facing the sun, shunning the light
the undersides of eyelids simmer red.

Fire isn't the only thing which sears
pressure applied by gentle hands leaves red.

Caricatures who breathe

The young man who draws caricatures
with both hands, can see people,
but something in his persona
stops him from actually seeing people,

with both hands, he can see people
who answer the same questions,
which stop him from actually seeing
people, who wait in the line,

who answer the same questions
in the same ways, passively—
people, who wait in the line
to see themselves blurred

in the same ways, passively
remarking on the accuracy
to see themselves blurred
by the re-marking of ink

remarking on the accuracy
that a stranger who recreates
by the re-marking of ink,
and the pausing of shadows

by a stranger who recreates—
but something in his persona
pauses, the shadows that frame
the young man, who is now a caricature.

In the middle

like the double sun
in the bus window

piercing one transparent wall
bouncing off the next
missing the original mark

you are doubled over

CREATIVE GATEWAY

LYNSEY NG
D'MANI THOMAS
BREANNA MISCIONE

CREATIVE GATEWAY

As we honor a wide range of Creative Discovery, we also want to recognize that such triumphs depend upon a creative foundation. At Berkeley, we seek to provide many points of entry to our creative culture, including "Creative Gateway" courses that introduce students to a range of arts and design forms while providing access to performances, exhibitions, and screenings throughout our incredible campus. Below we share sample reflections from students in one such course—Thinking Through Arts + Design at Berkeley: California Counter-Cultures. Whether describing a first experience in the theater or reckoning with the generational differences in our political landscape, they show our commitment to define, debate, and redefine what it means for UC Berkeley to propel creativity for the greater good.

Lynsey Ng

A time stamped review of Alvin Ailey's American Dance Theater from a snarky student who didn't want to be there. Equal parts insightful and sarcastic, the writer's inspired use of inset quotations, photo captioning and sentence fragments simultaneously lends and dismantles her credibility as an aloof twenty-something college student.

Lynsey Ng
B.A. Media Studies, 2018

Faculty Mentors: Natasha Boas, Independent Curator and Critic; Michael Cohen, African American Studies
Thinking Across the Arts + Design: California Countercultures

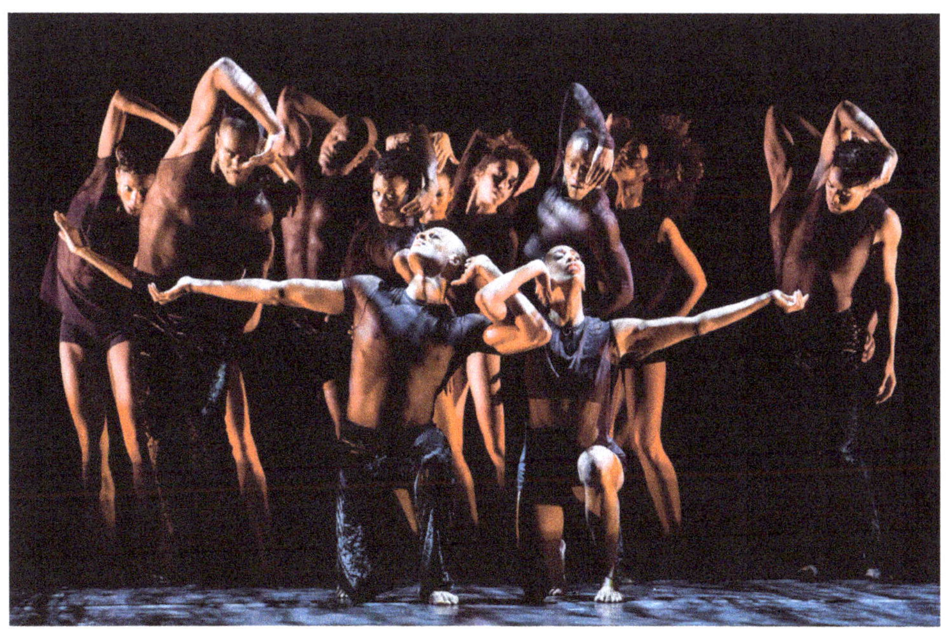

Exploring Alvin Ailey's Countercultural Dance Theater

I wanted to be celebrating Pi Day. With a pepperoni pizza on my couch in the quiet of my apartment.

I wanted to be celebrating Pi Day, but instead I'm strolling into Zellerbach Hall for my second Cal Performances event, Alvin Ailey's American Dance Theater. While the first was confusing and musically way over my head, this one proved to be stimulating and entertaining. *To be clear, I mean no disrespect to Steve Reich, but his music was more complex than the untrained ear (mine) could understand upon first listen.*

While I very much enjoyed the performance, I didn't walk in thinking that I would. So, as I am wont to do, I took notes of my experience so that I could turn it into something entertaining for myself later.

But as I came to find out, Alvin Ailey's American Dance Theater was actually a really powerful performance of counterculture.

Through and through, every element seemed to push back at the classical ballet.

Upon arriving at this realization, and still being in possession of my observation notes, I am instead pleased to present a live review of Alvin Ailey's American Dance Theater. Time stamps are sporadic because I only checked at intermissions and/or when I remembered.

Anyway, here it goes:

7:34 p.m.

Arrival. With time to spare too! Wow, student of the year.

My seat is on the balcony level, which is a nicer name for the nosebleeds. Hey, I don't mind. I didn't pay for this ticket, so I'll sit wherever they put me.

My seat is pretty high up, but it offers a killer view of the entire stage. I'm squarely in the middle of the auditorium with an unobstructed view. Can't complain.

8:00 p.m.

Almost showtime. Looks pretty close to a full house and the audience is buzzing as it does when there's a bar on the mezzanine level and the patrons arrived early enough to take full advantage.

Classic theater warning light dim.

It's. About. To go. Down. (Kevin Hart voice)

8:38 p.m.

First intermission. As in, there are multiple, apparently. But I'm not itching to leave, which is a bit of an interesting twist.

This is not the stuffy affair that I expected. The music is powerful with a strong beat, which makes a huge difference.

It's interesting how this first piece, *Deep*, acted as a countercultural foil to the classical ballet while also maintaining some familiar elements.

Familiar: There is something so satisfying about a group of people moving in perfect concert. Every kick of the leg, flourish of the hand and toss of the head is perfectly orchestrated and precisely choreographed. My Type-A perfectionist side takes a sick amount of satisfaction in this.

Countercultural: Most obviously, the music. Heavy, beat-driven and paired with powerful lyrics, this was not the stringed instrumental that I was expecting. The next thing I noticed was the dancers themselves. In addition to being almost entirely people of color—not something you see in classical ballet—they were clad in loose black tops and moved freely and fluidly—a far cry from the leotards and tense exactitude of ballet recitals.

The biggest indicator that I'm enjoying the performance is that when the curtain came down and the dancers bowed to the audience, 1. I did not immediately leave, and 2. I felt disappointed that the performance might be over already.

9:37 p.m.

Second intermission.

This one, *Walking Mad*, was interesting. It started with an undeniably fun number that engaged most of the cast. Where the first act was ethereal and somber, this one was bursting with color and the hectic nature of dance numbers in musicals and stage productions.

While vastly different from the first, this piece again counters the expectation of a well-behaved, typical dance production.

The music was upbeat with horn instruments and an infectiously catchy beat, matched with looser (and at times, comedic) choreography and flowy costuming. As important as the music was, the silence was even more so. At one point the jovial music cut off abruptly, causing the audience to think there was a technical issue when in fact it was simply part of the show. Even this, resisting the typical flow of a performance, proved to be a countercultural act.

Again, the illumination of the stage and dancers is very telling in the mood and tone of the piece. The golden-orange is for more somber pieces, while the blues and pinks are more light-hearted.

Walking Mad's use of physical props, most notably the wall unit, changed the composition of the stage and allowed dancers to change clothes and enter/exit from different places. It also skewed the vertical and horizontal axes and facilitated shadow play.

All of these elements were a reaction against the "classical", the "conventional", the "expected" that has come to characterize the classical ballet.

10:06 p.m.

This isn't an intermission, but a "pause" per the playbill.

Ella was a touching nod to Ella Fitzgerald. Again, the lighting plays a huge part in evoking certain emotions and setting the scene and mood.

The tribute was backed by Fitzgerald's distinctive "scat singing", which made it at times uncomfortable to listen to and unpleasing to the ear. This willingness to play unconventional, dissonant music again harkened to the performance's roots in counterculture.

The oft-discordant sounds were matched by the dancing duo's kinetic, percussive performance. I'm not sure if it's because those two did more cardio in that brief performance than I have in the last nine months, or because of the sheer power and conviction with which they moved, but *Ella* took my breath away.

10:29 p.m.

After eight bows from the dancers (and a wholly unsurprising ~spontaneous~, but nevertheless enjoyable, encore performance), the curtain finally drops and the house lights come up.

Parting Thoughts:

Alvin Ailey's American Dance Theater was much more entertaining than I expected.

Far from the stuffy affair I dreaded, this performance challenged convention at every place imaginable, from the bodies shown, to the music played, to the choreography danced and the audience targeted.

But at the same time, as with all countercultural movements, it also maintained the conventional structure of a classical, stage dance performance. It followed enough that the audience could recognize it as an art form requiring high levels of precision and expertise, while also rebelling against those very notions.

The dancers have wholly divorced themselves of the stiff, white, conventional narrative of traditional ballet, while managing to distill all the essential parts of such performances into a stage production that is completely their own.

Capturing this dichotomy, dwelling in this space that's very clearly not one nor the other, is an art form in itself and one that Alvin Ailey's American Dance Theater has perfected.

Fin.

Lynsey Ng, *Exploring Alvin Ailey's Countercultural Dance Theater*, 2017. 1200 words.

D'mani Thomas

Born from L&S 25 "California Counter Cultures," the piece explores the very awkward moment in which a black man catches himself being racist towards another black man. Through guest appearances from Brontez Purnell and Dena Beard, I discuss some of my more uncomfortable issues with museums and begin to re-understand black people and their relationship to space.

D'mani Thomas
B.A. Media Studies and African American Studies, 2018

Faculty Mentors: Natasha Boas, Independent Curator and Critic;
Michael Cohen, African American Studies
Thinking Across the Arts + Design: California Countercultures

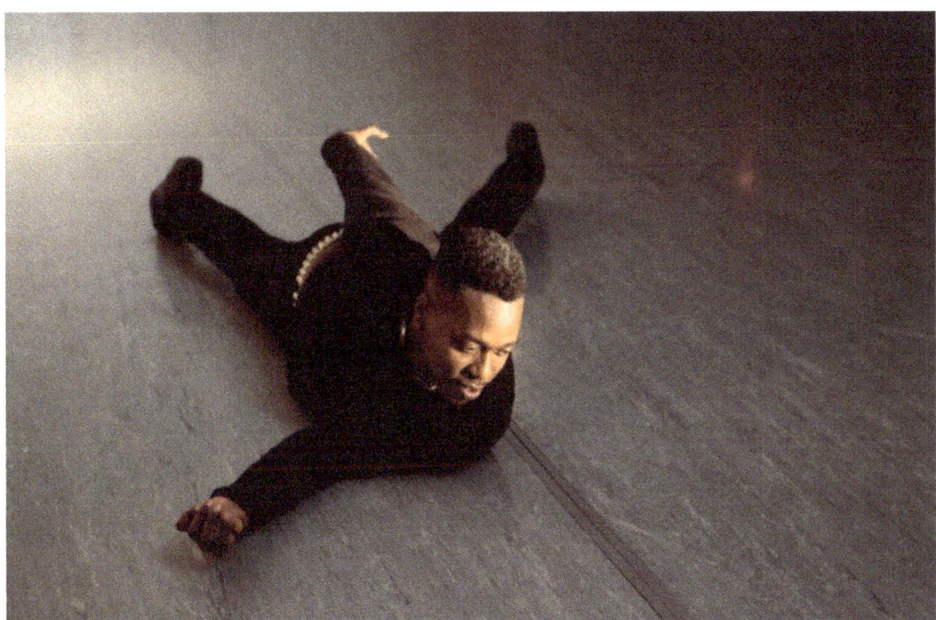

Poor timing, Brontez and Space

Important information before you read: *I am Black*

I walked into the Berkeley Art Museum. It was a normal day: I skipped a few classes, watched YouTube due to waking up late for said classes, drank some water and ate some cereal. But... when I walked into the lecture hall in the back of the art museum that Wednesday, I was met with a very interesting sight.

It may have been my internalized American racism, but when I saw a shirtless and shoe less black man reaching into a crowd of predominantly white and Asian people, I immediately became concerned for them. I thought, "Wow. Look at this homeless black man bothering these innocent students." The few seconds after these thoughts, I immediately checked myself and thought, "If you think of others like that, just off of a few seconds of information, what prevents others from thinking of you like that as well?" So, I kept observing the man, and quickly realized he was performing. The way he reached for the strings and walked on the bubble wrap became really fascinating to me. After he had left, I was left with one question:

What does it mean for this man to be allowed to do what he did and say what he did in a space like the Berkeley Art Museum?

I think of the Berkeley Art Museum as a white space. White space meaning: place that attracts a specific crowd because of its geographic location, content or atmosphere. The Berkeley Art Museum always has a squad of white patrons flooding in and out of its doors and due to its location within Berkeley, a town reflective of UC Berkeley's un-diverse admissions policies, I rarely get to see any people of color heading into the art museum. Brontez broke most of the preconceived notions I had of the art museum and made me feel a bit more comfortable within that space.

Our guest lecturer for the day was Dena Beard, director of The Lab. She introduced us to the concept of "Subjectile space": not just the surrounding environment for a work of art, but the support for said work of art... it is both acting and being acted upon. The example she used to try and help us understand that concept was "The Lab", alternative art space where artists are given complete creative. In this instance, The Lab is both a support for the artist's vision and is also the artist's vision.

Things that come to mind when I think of Subjectile Space:

- The maze from maze runner
- The wall and the giant concrete flower that had to be removed
- Music

I think of music because music creates space. If you walk into an ice-cream shop and hear: Jay Z's—"*Lost One*" then your perception of this ice cream shop as a space of delight may change. Music acts on us and is acted on by us. We place meaning onto different melodies and sonic waves. Music is its own supporting structure. Music only needs itself to create space. Even if you were outside, the right kind of music can turn a forest into the perfect prom setting (First *Twilight* Movie).

I did not get to ask Dena what she thought about this understanding of Subjectile Space and am curious to hear what she has to say given she has put more of her time into understanding this concept.

If we move forward with the understanding that music can create space, and black people have the ability to change a space just off of presence a lone, as shown through my perception of Brontez, then we understand subjectile space as a concept that can be attached to physical beings, and a bunch of different things other than just space.

I would like to thank Brontez and Dena for doing a lot for me that day. Things I am still processing and taking an appreciation for. Please visit "The Lab" (thelab.org) in case anyone is interested in visiting.

Breanna Miscione

Inspired by the teaching of the California Countercultures course (L&S 25), this work examines the context of social change from the mid-20th century and beyond. It then asks what social change means for us, especially millennials, in the age of technology and information. Accompanying the text is a collage of images from the various social movements that were discussed to illustrate the transformation of the artwork and methods of the movements.

Breanna Miscione
B.A. Psychology, 2019

Faculty Mentors: Natasha Boas, Independent Curator and Critic; Michael Cohen, African American Studies
Thinking Across the Arts + Design: California Countercultures

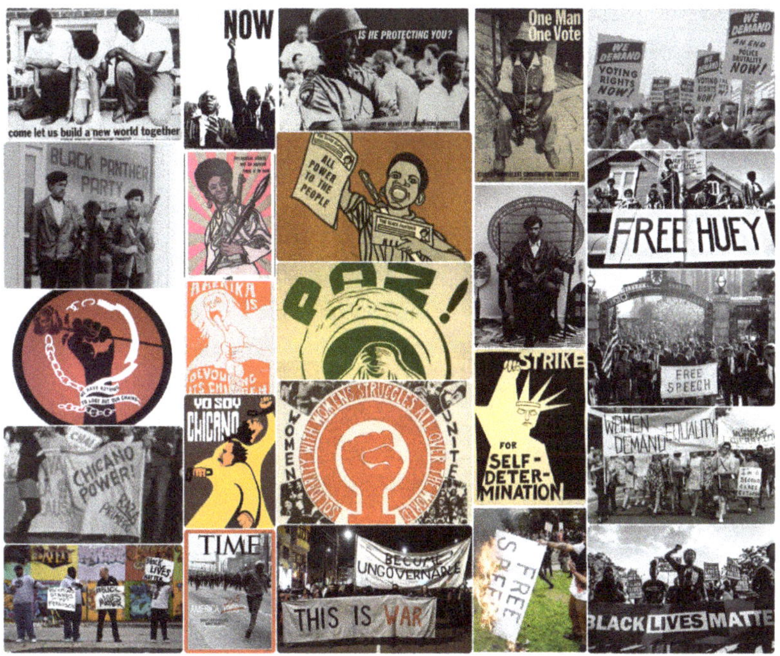

Conditions of Change

Taking time to examine the context of social change and what it means for us, especially millennials, in the age of technology and information.

> There comes a time when the operation of the machine becomes so odious, makes you so sick at heart, that you can't take part, you can't even passively take part, and you've got to put your bodies upon the gears and upon the wheels, upon all the apparatus, and you've got to make it stop. And you've got to indicate to the people who run it, the people who own it, that unless you're free the machine will be prevented from working at all
>
> —Mario Savio, 1964

Context, *noun*. The circumstances that form the setting for an event, statement, or idea, and in terms of which it can be fully understood and assessed.

I challenge you to think about the meaning of context and then describe the context of your last meal.

What did you describe as the "context?"

I just ate a burrito from a local taqueria in Berkeley. To fully understand this you would need to know why I was there, why the restaurant was there, and why I went to that restaurant. Things I could include in my explanation are the history of Mexico and California to explain the influences of Mexican culture within the state, my personal history as a SoCal native to explain why I chose a Mexican restaurant, information on our high achieving society that landed me in Berkeley to attend a high ranking university in hopes of gaining wealth later in life, the history of the restaurant owners to explain why they opened *this* restaurant and why *here*, and the history of Berkeley itself to explain how the intersections of these events was possible in the first place.

Too much information? Possibly. But where do we draw the line for what are "terms of which it can be fully understood and assessed?" My assumption is that we draw the line wherever it best suits our needs, but this is subjective. We see this flaw in the media when contextual lines are twisted and blurred to make a story that people want to hear. We also see this flaw in classrooms when "appropriate" becomes a self-serving tool.

Determining Context

We cannot understand where we are without knowing where we've been; we need to know the context. The social movements from the New Left and onward cannot be evaluated properly without discussing the Civil Rights Movement.

In 1960, the Student Nonviolent Coordinating Committee (SNCC) was founded in Greensboro, North Carolina. Its members, mostly students of color, aimed to create broad social change through use of propaganda and peaceful demonstrations such as sit-ins and marches. SNCC's propaganda utilized bold lettering and relatable images so that their message was clear and created an emotional reaction within the viewer. Very similar styles were used by Oakland's own Black Panther Party for Self Defense. The ideologies held by the Panthers were more radical than those held by SNCC, but the art they produced was effective in communicating their message. Perhaps SNCC's greatest legacy to the New Left was their grassroots method of organizing. They exhibited their efficacy in 1964 when they joined forces with other civil rights groups to direct The Freedom Summer in Mississippi.

SLATE, a political party established at UC Berkeley in 1958, aimed to increase student action towards external issues and was greatly influenced by the stirrings of the

Civil Right Movement. Beyond their political agenda, they worked to teach students how to think and organize independently, much like the grassroots operations of SNCC. Mario Savio, a member of SLATE, attended the Freedom Summer in 1964. What he saw influenced him to contribute to the growing Free Speech Movement on campus at UC Berkeley. His involvement culminated in his speech in front of Sproul Hall, a quintessential moment for the Movement.

The New Left continued to flourish on UC Berkeley's campus, and beyond, throughout the 1970s as the Anti-war Movement, Chicano Movement, and Women's Liberation Movement among others continued. During this time, Wurster Hall had been completely taken over by student groups and turned into a poster-making factory producing mostly anti-war propaganda along with other disobedient artwork. You can see the influence of the Civil Rights Movement and the psychedelic nature of the growing counterculture movement in their artwork and environmentally friendly practices. It's a fact that we often draw from and reappropriate the actions of others.

Now

We can't know where we are going without knowing where we are; again, we need to know the context.

Times have changed. We have new technologies, complicated politics, a split nation, an increasing gap between the rich and the poor, a decrease in need for unskilled labor, increases of college tuition, and the list goes on. I can say one thing for sure, the New Left is dead for two reasons: prices and technology.

A 'sensible' student would never put themselves in a situation that would jeopardize the education that they're paying a quarter of a million dollars for. But as millennials, we would gladly post a video of other people rioting or being beat up or arrested. We'd then count how many views our video got and compare that to our friends'. I have seen firsthand students posting/ranting on Facebook about how they "couldn't believe what they saw" and how "this is what's wrong with America" (believe me, I've heard it from both sides) but the live videos they posted the night before proved they did absolutely nothing but stand an ample distance away and film whatever they disapproved of. Now we have the ability to hide behind computer screens and we are likely to do it because the costs are literally too high to do otherwise.

Today on campus there are no spaces dedicated towards social action to the same extent as Wurster Hall was in the 70s. Today, space must be used "efficiently," and that means more classrooms, more labs, and more offices. It's representative of both our high achieving culture and our political apathy as a nation. We no longer have the drive to produce social change like we used to on college campuses.

Where do we go from here?

So where are we going?! I'm not really sure but I can bet that technology is the force that will take us there. E-news, e-mails, blogs, status updates, photos, live videos, you name it, are all methods by which social movements organize and disperse their message in today's world. While technology is becoming the platform by which the world operates, we still incorporate many of the tactics utilized by those of the Civil Right Movements and New Left during the Long Sixties.

We are at a critical point in history as these two forces combine and we have the potential to revive the fervor for social justice that has dwindled in our country. And we can succeed, but we must understand the context of social change in order to make one.

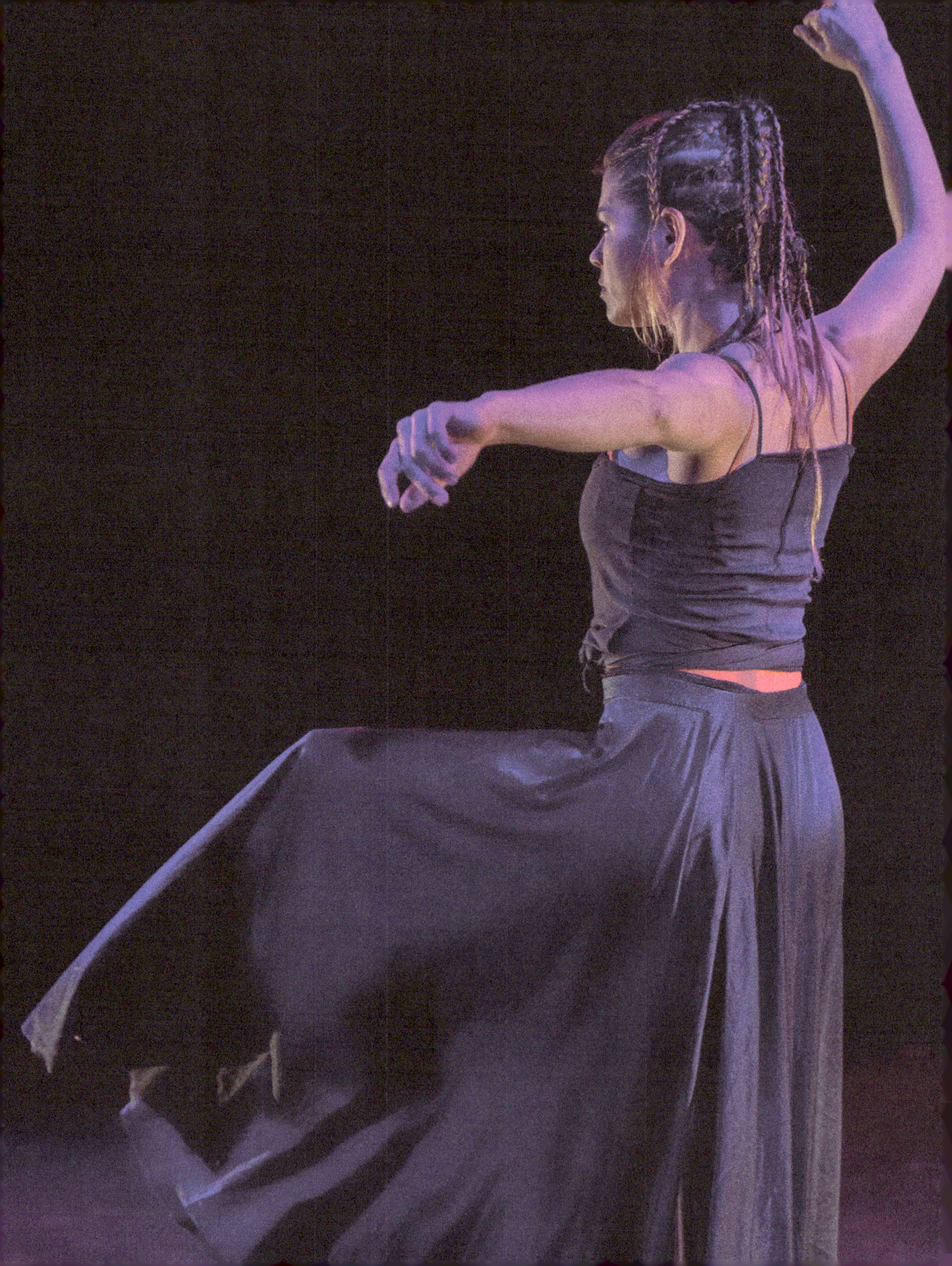

INDEX

NEW CLASSICS

Alexander Barreira, English (2018); Faculty Mentor: Jeffrey Knapp, English

Edoardo Benzoni, Theater, Dance, and Performance Studies (2017); Faculty Mentor: Lura Dolas, Theater, Dance, and Performance Studies

Jin Young Jun, History of Art (2017); Faculty Mentor: Henrike Lange, History of Art

Merissa Mann, Art Practice (2017); Faculty Mentor: Jean Paul Bourdier, College of Environmental Design

Andrew Rahman, Music (2017); Faculty Mentor: Edmund Campion, Music

Jenny Rempert, Architecture (2020); Faculty Mentor: Henrike Lange, History of Art

Theodora Serbanescu-Martin, English & Music (2016); Faculty Mentor: Nicholas Mathew, Music

Maya Shen, Cognitive Science (2020); Faculty Mentor: Henrike Lange, History of Art

PUBLIC WORKS

The Renegade Classroom Team: Ryan Alexander, Sustainable Environmental Design (2017), Can Ceyhan, Sustainable Environmental Design (2017), Oriya Cohen, Sustainable Environmental Design (2017), Lila Frisher, Sustainable Environmental Design (2017), Jess Schaefer, Sustainable Environmental Design (2017); Faculty Mentor: Emily Pilloton, College of Environmental Design

Aurore Develay, Landscape Architecture and Environmental Planning (2018); Faculty Mentor: Jennifer Brooks, College of Environmental Design

Cecelia DiMino, Linguistics (2018); Faculty Mentor: Phillip Denny, Blum Center for Developing Economics

Bishal Dutta, Film and Media Studies (2018); Faculty Mentor: Linda Williams, Film & Media

PUBLIC WORKS (cont.)

Aboubacar Komara, Architecture (2018); Faculty Mentor: Juliana Raimondi, College of Environmental Design

James Payne, English (2017); Faculty Mentors: Geoffrey O'Brien, English, Robert Hass, English, John Shoptaw, English

Ian Sheerin, English (2018); Faculty Mentor: Eric Falci, English

Zhifei Xu, Architecture (2017); Faculty Mentor: Rene Davids, College of Environmental Design

FRIENDS AND STRANGERS

Amanda Team: Aidee Cantu, Cognitive Science (2017), Mane Chakarian, Psychology & Interdisciplinary Studies (2017), Jiachen Hu, Computer Science (2017), Taylor Wong, Electrical Engineering and Computer Science (2018); Faculty Mentor: James Pierce, Jacobs Institute for Design Innovation

Paige Davis, Art Practice & American Studies (2017) & Weston Smith, Art Practice (2017); Faculty Mentor: Allan deSouza, Art Practice

Kyler Ernst, English (2018); Faculty Mentor: Namwali Serpell, English

Farrah Kazemi, Film Studies (2017); Faculty Mentor: J. Mira Koppell, Film & Media

Adam Mansour, Anthropology (2017), Faculty Mentor: Terrence Deacon, Anthropology

Shrinking Violets Team: Kate Masancay, Media Studies (2017), Sebastian Ospina, Cognitive Science (2017), Shota Pangilinan, Cognitive Science (2017), Sharon Wang, Media Studies (2018), Peggy Zhao, Cognitive Science (2017); Faculty Mentor: Sara Beckman, Haas School of Business

Bennett Shaeffer, Undeclared (2019); Faculty Mentor: Rama Gottfried, Music

LIVING OBJECTS

Smart Home Devices for the Blind Team: Arshad Ali, Computer Science (2017), Alex Chong, Mechanical Engineering & Electrical Engineering and Computer Science (2017), Stephen Chu, Mechanical Engineering (2017), Yudi Sun, Sociology (2018); Faculty Mentor: Euiyoung Kim, Jacobs Institute for Design Innovation

Jason Bircea, English (2017); Faculty Mentor: Celeste Langan, English

Aileen Candelario, Art Practice & Journalism (2018); Faculty Mentor: Azin Seraj, Art Practice

Farm to Label Team: Ziqi Chen, Computer Science (2019), Chengcheng Huang, Master's in Architecture (2018), Carlo Liquido, Master of Science in Information and Management Systems (2017), Shail Shah, Master's in Engineering (2017), Michael Singer, Master's in Engineering (2017); Faculty Mentor: Eric Paulos, Electrical Engineering and Computer Science

Belinda Cortez, Art Practice (2017); Faculty Mentor: Brody Reiman, Art Practice

Principal Power Buoy Team: Hunter Garnier, Mechanical Engineering (2018), Stephanie Mah, Mechanical Engineering (2017), Akhilesh Mishra, Mechanical Engineering (2018), Beshoy Wabha, Mechanical Engineering (2018), Alexander Wing, Economics (2018), Albert Zhou, Mechanical Engineering (2018); Faculty Mentor: Euiyoung Kim, Jacobs Institute for Design Innovation

Sasha Kudler, Music & English (2017); Faculty Mentor: Jeffrey Blevins, English

Fetal and Maternal Health Monitoring Team: Tushar Mittal, Chemical Biology & Material Science (2018), Arbaaz Shakir, Mechanical Engineering (2018); Faculty Mentor: Euiyoung Kim, Jacobs Institute for Design Innovation

Jerome Rivera Pansa, Art Practice (2017); Faculty Mentors: Brody Reiman, Art Practice & Anne Walsh, Art Practice

Katie Revilla, Art Practice (2017); Faculty Mentor: Allan deSouza, Art Practice

INSIDE AND OUT

Lights in Tensegrity (LiT) Team: Patrick Angelo, Mechanical Engineering (2018), Jocelyn Kim, Chemical Engineering (2018), Vineet Nair, Mechanical Engineering & Economics (2018), Nicole Parker, Mechanical Engineering (2017), Alvin Tan, Mechanical Engineering (2018); Faculty Mentor: Euiyoung Kim, Jacobs Institute for Design Innovation

Katherine Basu, Theater, Dance, and Performance Studies (2017); Faculty Mentor: Jack Carpenter, Theater, Dance, and Performance Studies

Gabe Carr, Art Practice (2017); Faculty Mentors: Allan deSouza, Art Practice & Randy Hussong, Art Practice

WheelSense Team: Tomas Vega Galvez, Computer Science & Cognitive Science (2017), Corten Singer Winger, Computer Science & Cognitive Science (2017); Faculty Mentors: Edward Lee, Electrical Engineering and Computer Science & Björn Hartmann, Electrical Engineering and Computer Science & Jacobs Institute for Design Innovation

Mollie Sitzer, Landscape Architecture (2016); Faculty Mentor: Chip Sullivan, College of Environmental Design

Arvin Tanu, Architecture (2017); Faculty Mentor: Jean Paul Bourdier, College of Environmental Design

Kristen Wilson, English & American Studies (2017); Faculty Mentor: George Starr, English

Zhoushu Ziporyn, Music & Philosophy (2017); Faculty Mentor: Ken Ueno, Music

IDENTITIES AND TRANSITIONS

Replika Team: Patrick Burden, Business Administration (2017), Miranda Clemmons, Cognitive Science (2017), Sebastian Ospina, Cognitive Science (2017), Shota Pangilinan, Cognitive Science (2017); Faculty Mentor: James Pierce, Jacobs Institute for Design Innovation

Whitewashing Machine Team: Patrick Burden, Business Administration (2017), Danielle Kenwood, Cognitive Science (2017), Carlo Liquido, Master of Science in Information and Management Systems (2017), Isabel Wang, Architecture (2018), Alex Sung, Computer Science (2017); Faculty Mentor: Jill Miller, Berkeley Center for New Media

Gabriel Cazares, Film and Media Studies (2017); Faculty Mentor: J. Mira Kopell, Film & Media

ReEmploy Team: Serena Chang, Electrical Engineering and Computer Science (2017), Michael Chen, Computer Science (2017), Nikhil Patel, Computer Science (2018), Audrey Tsai, Cognitive Science & Computer Science (2017); Faculty Mentors: Björn Hartmann, Jacobs Institute for Design Innovation & Zvika Krieger, Jacobs Institute for Design Innovation

Irene Chen, Art Practice, Rhetoric, & Film Studies (2017); Faculty Mentor: J. Mira Koppell, Film & Media

Madeline Kresin, English (2018); Faculty Mentor: David A. Miller, English

Moira Laband, Film and Media Studies & Psychology (2017); Faculty Mentor: J. Mira Koppell, Film & Media

Sahvanna Mazon, English (2017); Faculty Mentors: Ken Mahru, English & Lyn Hejinian, English

GATEWAYS TO CREATIVITY AT BERKELEY

Breanna Miscione, Psychology (2019); Faculty Mentors: Natasha Boas, Independent Curator and Critic, Michael Cohen, African American Studies, *Thinking Across the Arts + Design: California Countercultures*

Lynsey Ng, Media Studies (2018); Faculty Mentors: Natasha Boas, Independent Curator and Critic, Michael Cohen, African American Studies, *Thinking Across the Arts + Design: California Countercultures*

D'mani Thomas, Media Studies & African American Studies (2018); Faculty Mentors: Natasha Boas, Independent Curator and Critic, Michael Cohen, African American Studies, *Thinking Across the Arts + Design: California Countercultures*

With special thanks to Sara Martinez, Susan Miller, Paris Cotz, Lauren Pearson, Amber Fogarty, Soomin Suh, Sarah Fullerton Dragovich and all the students and faculty who made this beautiful compilation possible.

Berkeley Arts + Design

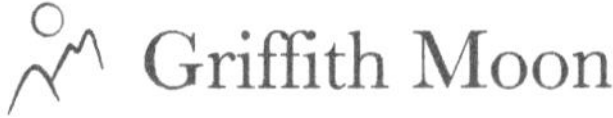

www.ingramcontent.com/pod-product-compliance
Lightning Source LLC
LaVergne TN
LVHW070928160826
845679LV00017B/1754
9780999845233